FANCY YOUR CHANCES?

MURDEROUS MATHS

DO YOU FEEL LUCKY?

Kjartan Poskitt

illustrated by Philip Reeve

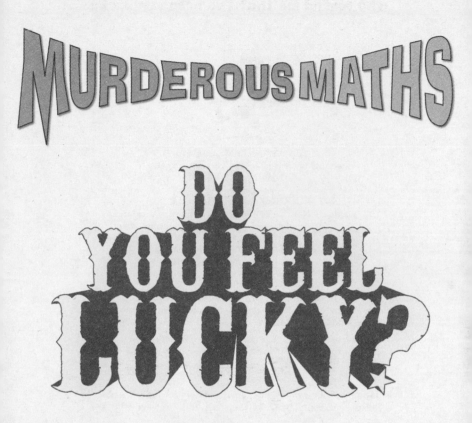

MURDEROUS MATHS

DO YOU FEEL LUCKY?

**To Bridget, Maisie, Florence, Dulcie and Miranda
who remind me that I've been very lucky.**

Scholastic Children's Books,
Euston House, 24 Eversholt Street,
London NW1 1DB, UK

A division of Scholastic Ltd
London ~ New York ~ Toronto ~ Sydney ~ Auckland
Mexico City ~ New Delhi ~ Hong Kong

First published in the UK by Scholastic Ltd, 2001
This edition published 2010

ISBN 978 1407 10712 7

Page layout services provided by Quadrum Solutions Plc, Mumbai, India
Printed and bound by CPI Group (UK) Ltd, Croydon, CR0 4YY

15

Contents

One day in the forgotten desert

The vultures gently hovered high above the entrance to the cave while outside in the blinding sunlight, the two barbarian armies nursed their swords and axes in silence. None of them would admit it, but some days being a barbarian simply wasn't as much fun as they had come to expect.

The whole idea of being a barbarian was to take offence at something really pathetic, and then have a bloody fight for a few hours and finally wind down with a massive party. Both armies still recalled fondly the bone-crunching punch-up that came after Gorgo the Orgo suggested that Mungoid the Jungoid was deliberately leaving his dustbins out across Gorgo's driveway.

The only disappointment was that by the time it came to the party, neither Gorgo nor Mungoid had anybody to go with. Mind you, even though their bodies were missing, their heads still took the places of honour on large silver dishes at the top table.

But this argument had been different. Urgum the
Axeman and Grizelda the Grisly had been sorting
out their scalp collections, and both had decided
they needed one more – each other's.

For days the two armies had been practising their
most scary faces and blood-curdling war cries, but
when they finally came to meet up, Urgum took
Grizelda aside.

"This is too serious for a mere battle," he had said.

"Agreed," agreed Grizelda. "But how do we decide
who gets the other's scalp?"

"Come with me," said Urgum as he headed towards
the cave.

Waiting inside was a small man in a big hat.

"This is Thag, the mathemagician," said Urgum.
"His way is to throw the stone of six sides."

"We throw that little stone?" Grizelda had gasped
when she saw what the small man was holding.
"We'll never kill each other with that!"

"Nonetheless, many have died for it!" chuckled the small man. "Believe me, this little object contains more power and mystery than the greatest rock you could ever throw."

"'Tis a power stone!" gasped Grizelda and she instinctively leapt backwards.

"Not a power stone," said Thag as he rolled it around his hand to show off the six sides and the spots. "'Tis but a die."

"Die?" shouted Grizelda brandishing her triple-headed battleaxe. "If anyone dies around here it won't be me!"

"No no, the stone is called a die!" explained Thag hurriedly. "It's just the name. More than one of them are called dice, but just one is called a die."

After a moment's hesitation, Grizelda took the die then tossed it on to the floor.

"Aha!" grinned Thag. "The uppermost side bears the single spot. Now the dispute can be decided."

"How?" asked Grizelda.

"You must throw the die again and hope the single spot lands on top," explained Thag. "If so, you claim Urgum's scalp."

"And if not, then I claim yours," said Urgum.

"But there are six sides, and only one has the single spot!" said Grizelda.

"You may have three attempts," said Thag. "But if you fail in all three, your scalp goes to Urgum."

Grizelda thought long and hard, and as she did so she ran her fingers through her freshly washed, dandruff-free, pH-balanced, naturally conditioned locks. Boy, it would be a shame to lose them, but there again it would be so good to have Urgum's two metres of rope-like ponytail hanging over her fireplace.

I'VE ONE CHANCE IN SIX OF THROWING A SINGLE SPOT IN THE FIRST THROW. SO IN THREE THROWS THERE SHOULD BE THREE CHANCES IN SIX. IT SEEMS FAIR...

As Grizelda reached for the die, Thag stepped outside. A few minutes later there came a hideous scream from inside the cave. High above, the circling vultures started to drool.

"What was that?" asked one of the barbarians.

"Somebody just lost their scalp," replied another.

"Do you know who it was?" they asked Thag.

"I can't be certain," grinned Thag. "But I've a pretty good idea. Anybody fancy a little bet on it?"

PLACE YOUR BETS HERE

So what do YOU think?

Grizelda obviously thought the die game was fair, but was it? If it wasn't fair, then who is more likely to win – Grizelda or Urgum? There's only one way to get the answer...

Yahoo! Once again it's time to fasten your seat-belts, Murderous Maths fans, as we hack our way through another stretch of the maths jungle. Be warned though: this time we're taking things right to the very edge of sanity itself! As well as finding out who's likely to get scalped, we'll also investigate cards, snakes, birthdays, coins, aliens, pigeons, tricks and trousers ... oh, and we'll be conjuring up a few numbers big enough to give a computer convulsions. Are you ready for this? Then brace yourself as we delve into the diabolical, devious and deceptive world of...

– the most murderous part of maths. (Well. probably...)

Before we enter the strange world of probability...

...we need to start by learning some of the special language involved in probability. (For starters we're going to call it chance because probability is a bit of a mouthful.)

There is also one very simple but vital sum that we need and then by the end of this chapter you'll be ready for some of the strangest stuff you'll ever come across.

The main word is probably probably

The first job is to make sure we know what we're talking about. As chance comes up a lot in everyday life there are lots of different ways of describing it. For instance, all these questions are asking the same thing:

- What is the probability of Pongo McWhiffy turning up?
- What are the chances of Pongo McWhiffy turning up?
- What is the likelihood of Pongo McWhiffy turning up?
- What are the odds on Pongo McWhiffy turning up?
- What are the prospects of Pongo McWhiffy turning up?
- What's the risk of Pongo McWhiffy turning up?

And before we wonder too hard about it, here he is!

As ever, he's going to try his luck with the terribly lovely Veronica Gumfloss, so let's watch and enjoy a truly heartwarming tale of love, passion and romance.

As Pongo debates the outcome of this extraordinarily dangerous suggestion, we'll take this opportunity to develop our language skills.

Although Pongo's friends are all saying different things, they all mean the same. Knowing how fiercely Veronica protects her saint-like reputation, they all know that there is only one possible outcome to Pongo's advance. Let's get it over with.

Once again, take note of the profound observations
provided by Pongo's ever-supportive chums:

And let's see Veronica's reaction:

So far then, we've seen how to describe things that definitely will happen, and things that definitely will not. But suddenly Pongo finds an old unopened birthday card covered in fluff and old sweet papers in his anorak pocket.

All of a sudden nobody is certain! They think that the envelope probably won't contain any money, but this is where the fun starts. As soon as the word "probably"

turns up, we are talking about chance. In this case there's only a very small chance but who knows...

Here we're seeing some choice expressions that often occur when somebody has "beaten the odds" – in other words the chance of a happy outcome was very small but it "came up". Pongo immediately invests his cash wisely.

This is exciting stuff! Will Pongo's newfound wealth buy him a place in Veronica's heart? Nobody can guess at the outcome – in fact the kid who says "it's a toss up" is saying the situation is similar to tossing a coin which is just as likely to land on heads as it is tails. But today Pongo is in luck because fate takes a hand.

It looks good, and in fact – yes! – Veronica is getting into the taxi, but...

During the course of this book we'll be coming across all these expressions and seeing how they describe the exact level of chance involved. Off we go then and we'll start with the simplest sort of chance there is.

The toss up

Tossing a coin is the fastest and surest way of deciding between two choices. This can affect the outcome of some major events, especially in sport. Although players train for years to be stars at football, cricket and the hopping marathon, before the starting whistle is blown, a coin gets tossed. Even the best players in the world have to stand by and watch helplessly as the little coin decides which end the teams play at, who bats first or which leg is to be used for the 26-mile hopathon.

The reason a coin is used is that it is very simple and very fair. It's simple because there are only two possible results – heads or tails. More importantly, it's fair because the coin doesn't care which side it lands on, and what's really hard to understand is that *the coin has no memory*. What a funny thing to say, eh? We'll see why many people think that coins do have memories later on, but first let's check on what happens when you toss a coin.

PING!

Let's switch gravity off for a moment and leave the coin up in the air. (With Murderous Maths we can do stuff like that. Isn't it great?) Before we let the coin land, we have to guess what the *outcome* will be, in other words will it land "heads" or "tails"?

Here's our first bit of maths. If we want to describe the chance of *anything* happening you make a fraction like this:

$$\text{chance} = \frac{\text{number of useful outcomes}}{\text{number of possible outcomes}}$$

With tossing a coin we have two possible outcomes: "heads" or "tails". If we want "heads" then we only have one useful outcome. So the chance of tossing heads $= \frac{1}{2}$. This fraction tells us that if you toss the coin lots of times, you can expect the coin to land on heads about half of those times.

Right, let's switch gravity back on again and see if it's heads.

And why not? Tails is the other possible outcome and so the chance of tails is also $\frac{1}{2}$. Of course we'd expect the chance of tails to be the same as the chance of heads because there's nothing on a normal coin that can make it land on one side more than the other. Sometimes you win, sometimes you lose and there's nothing you can do about it.

So if the coin lands on heads OR tails, you win?

Oh well, if you're going to be like that...

$$\text{chance} = \frac{2 \text{ useful outcomes}}{2 \text{ possible outcomes}} = \frac{2}{2} = 1$$

Or we could say that the chance of getting heads is $\frac{1}{2}$ and the chance of tails is also $\frac{1}{2}$. As you can only get heads or tails but not both at the same time, the clever way of describing these outcomes is to call them **mutually exclusive**. We're allowed to add up the chances of mutually exclusive outcomes, so in this case we get $\frac{1}{2} + \frac{1}{2} = 1$.

IT CAME DOWN TAILS! I WIN! I'M SO BRILLIANT!

Well of course he won. The coin definitely had to land on either heads or tails, it was a sure thing, a dead cert. Most importantly, it was *a chance of 1* and this fact is so important that it's about to get a few pages all to itself...

When one is a dead cert

The vital sum that comes up in chance is so simple you could kiss it. We've just seen what it is, but we'll check it again:

> **The chances of all the different outcomes must add up to 1.**

When we tossed a coin, there were only two possible outcomes and they each had a chance of $\frac{1}{2}$. Add them together and you get $\frac{1}{2}+\frac{1}{2}=1$.

TWO QUICK TIPS WITH FRACTIONS:
- If you're adding fractions that have the same number on the bottom, you just add the tops together. So $\frac{1}{2}+\frac{1}{2}=\frac{1+1}{2}=\frac{2}{2}$. In the same way $\frac{2}{7}+\frac{3}{7}=\frac{5}{7}$.
- If a fraction has the same number on both top and bottom, the fraction equals 1. So $\frac{2}{2}=1$.

These two tips are almost all you need to work out chance sums, but if there's anything more you want to know about fractions, it's all in *The Mean And Vulgar Bits*.

Tree diagrams and saving the universe

One way of seeing how chances work is by drawing out a "tree diagram". It's worth reading the next bits very carefully...

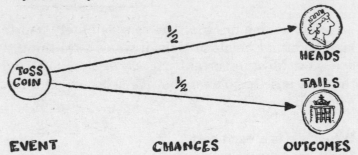

- The diagram always starts with an "event" such as tossing a coin, then it has lines (also called "branches") coming off the event to show all the different outcomes. Soon we'll see how these outcomes can lead on to other events such as

22

tossing a second coin, but just for now we'll keep it nice and simple.

- All the outcomes connected to an event are described as mutually exclusive – if one outcome happens, then another cannot. If a coin lands on heads, it can't land on tails at the same time, so these outcomes are mutually exclusive. The good thing about mutually exclusive outcomes is that we can add them to each other, and you'll see why this is useful in a minute.

- The chances of each outcome are marked on the branch and *all the chances connected to the same event must add up to 1*. With our simple "toss coin" event we get $\frac{1}{2}+\frac{1}{2}=1$.

Once you've understood these three points, you'll find that tree diagrams can deal with almost any situation, even when you happen to be holding a normal die and the evil Gollarks from the planet Zog drop by for a little chat.

THROW A FOUR OR WE'LL DESTROY THE ENTIRE UNIVERSE!

They do enjoy their fun, don't they? Bless 'em. So what are the chances?

The die has six sides which means there are six possible outcomes each with a chance of $\frac{1}{6}$.

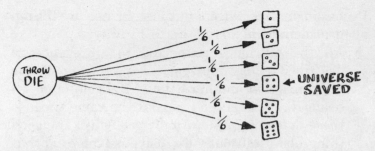

As the tree diagram shows, only one outcome will save the universe, so the chance is $\frac{1}{6}$.

What are the chances that we *don't* get a four? There are five sides on the die that *don't* give us a four and each of these outcomes has a chance of $\frac{1}{6}$. As these outcomes are mutually exclusive we can add them up, so we find the chances of not getting a four are $\frac{1}{6}+\frac{1}{6}+\frac{1}{6}+\frac{1}{6}+\frac{1}{6}=\frac{5}{6}$. Now we can make the diagram a bit simpler because if we don't get a four, we won't really care what the outcome is because the universe will come to an end.

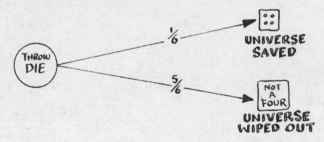

What are the chances that we will either get a four or NOT get a four? We add together the two chances $\frac{1}{6}+\frac{5}{6}$ and get the answer $\frac{6}{6}$. This is the same as 1 which means the chance is a dead cert. Well of course it is! If you throw a die, you'll either get a four or you won't – there's no other possible outcome!

It doesn't matter what sort of event you're talking about, this rule of adding up to 1 always applies.

Pigeon probability

Suppose you are a pigeon flying over a station platform and you suddenly decide that you've GOT TO GO. If you just shut your eyes and let it drop, what are the chances that you splatter a man or a woman? Believe it or not, you can work this out (if you happen to be an extremely intelligent pigeon).

Let's assume that if the platform was completely jammed full, it has enough space to hold 200 people. You could do your worst now, and be absolutely sure of splatting somebody, because there is no chance of missing! However, if there were only 199 people on the platform, it would mean there was one empty place. This means you only have 199 useful outcomes from the 200 possible outcomes. So there's 1 chance out of 200 of missing completely. What a waste.

As it turns out, when you fly overhead, you see that the platform only has 40 men and 25 women on it. The rest of the platform (which could have held 135 people) is just empty space.

You have 40 chances out of 200 of splatting a man! We can write this as $\frac{40}{200}$. (If you're good at fractions you might be tempted immediately to cancel this down to $\frac{1}{5}$, but with chance sums it's a lot easier to wait until the very end.)

You have 25 chances out of 200 of splatting a woman or $\frac{25}{200}$. (Yes fraction freaks, this would cancel down to $\frac{1}{8}$, but try to resist the temptation!)

What are your chances of splatting a man OR a woman? We just add up $\frac{40}{200} + \frac{25}{200}$ and get the chance of splatting a man or a woman as $\frac{65}{200}$. (If you DID cancel down the first two fractions, you'd now have to add $\frac{1}{5} + \frac{1}{8}$ to get $\frac{13}{40}$. A nasty little sum which serves you right for trying to be too clever.)

BUT I THOUGHT THE TOTAL CHANCES WERE SUPPOSED TO MAKE 1?

What you have to do is make sure you've thought of all the possible outcomes. So far we've only dealt with two of them – you could splat a man, or you could splat a woman. The third outcome is that you could miss completely, so let's see what the chances are of hitting one of the 135 empty spaces. Simple, it's $\frac{135}{200}$.

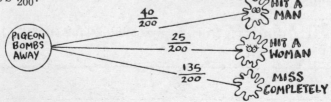

Once again we can add up the outcomes because they're mutually exclusive (of the three possibilities, the pigeon can only get one of them). This means we can add the three chances up and find that:

$$\frac{40}{200} + \frac{25}{200} + \frac{135}{200} = \frac{40+25+135}{200} = \frac{200}{200} = 1.$$

SO EVEN IF YOU'RE BIRD-BRAINED, ALL THE OUTCOMES MUST ADD UP TO 1

CALCULATOR AMNESTY

Normally in Murderous Maths we think that calculators are just for wimps and losers, but we do appreciate that chance involves working out an unfair amount of ugly stuff. Therefore the Murderous Maths organization have promised not to come round and bang on your door or pull faces at your window if you use a calculator for chance sums.

Later on there's a lot of big numbers to be multiplied and divided, so do feel free to swallow your pride and push a few buttons. We understand.

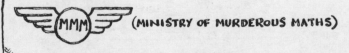 (MINISTRY OF MURDEROUS MATHS)

How not to lose your trousers

You know what it's like. Somebody called Legsy Johnson comes up to you and says something like, "I can lick my ears," and you immediately reply, "I bet you can't," and Legsy says, "What do you bet then?" and you say, "I bet my trousers," and then Legsy licks her ears and the next thing you know, you have to walk home with no trousers on.

The trouble is, it was so unlikely that Legsy could lick her ears, you felt that your trousers were going to be yours for ever. There's an important lesson to learn from this: if somebody comes up to you and offers to bet on something really silly, maybe they know something you don't. Don't bet!

Why some people won't like this book
A lot of people will think that if you're reading a book about chance, then you might be encouraged to "gamble" which can end up costing you a massive amount of money – not to mention losing your trousers. However, if you read this book carefully, you'll realize that gambling isn't such a clever thing to do, as Binky Smallbrains will now demonstrate.

WHAT HO!

Why slot machines are GUARANTEED to make you look stupid

One of the easiest and silliest ways to start gambling is when you see a nice shiny flashy slot machine.

Providing that you're old enough and it's your money *and you don't need it for anything else*, then it all seems harmless enough – but before you start feeding the coins in, have a good look at the machine. It's full of electronics, has lots of groovy lights and buttons and it comes in a nice big box with pretty coloured glass, so what do you think it cost to make? £1,000? £2,000? More? Now think about this – why would anybody want to spend thousands of pounds on making a slot machine if it was just going to pass money out to anyone who fancied playing it?

Don't be silly, Binky. Slot machines swallow up far more money than they pay out and they will swallow up your money too. This will make you feel a bit stupid, and for most people that's enough. When you've had your money's worth of being stupid you can toddle off and decide that in future you'll spend money on more rewarding things.

Well done, Binky. Now you are being even more stupid because you are starting to use money that you don't really have. Why are you doing it? Do you think…

- it must be the machine's turn to hand over some money?
- the machine will be feeling sorry for you?
- the machine is so full of cash that it can't hold any more so some has to leak out soon?

Be honest Binky, one of these three thoughts must be buzzing round that empty bean can that you use as a brain. It's pitiful to watch.

Although you are being stupid, the machine is rather clever. Occasionally it will tease you...

...and if you had any sense, you'd take the money and run.

It's scary to think what is passing through your little mind now, but it's probably along these lines:

- You know more about gambling than the machine does.
- The machine loves you more than anybody else.
- An invisible magic pixie is sitting on your shoulder and sprinkling you with lucky fairy dust.

So in your money goes – and not just your winnings but probably everything else you've got too.

Don't worry, Binky. Even when you've lost all your money, you can pretend you've had a good time because you got to see some flashing lights, you got to push some buttons and you heard some music playing. Aw diddums! Another time, why not go to a toy shop and get yourself one of those little baby activity games with lights, buttons and music? They last a lot longer and will save you a fortune.

Of course there are lots of other ways of gambling apart from slot machines, and all sorts of people can't resist having a go. The interesting thing about people who gamble a lot is that they have defective memories. If they win a lot of money on one day, they will talk about that day for months. But somehow, they always forget to tell you about all the many other days when they lost! Mind you, if they lose their trousers as well as their money – they can't very well pretend it didn't happen!

The man that broke the bank at Monte Carlo

In 1891 an Englishman called Charles Deville Wells made betting history. In July he went to the famous gambling resort at Monte Carlo and after three long days he had won about £1,000,000 in today's money. He went back in November and did the same thing again which made him famous all over the world and there were even songs written about him. However everybody seems to have forgotten that he went back again in 1892 and lost so much money that he ended up in prison. So how did the bank at

Monte Carlo feel about it? They were delighted because the publicity attracted loads more wealthy people desperate to throw their money away. What's more, even when Wells won they could easily afford to pay (he only "broke" one small part of their operation) and in the end he couldn't resist coming back and losing it all again!

JULY 1891 – BREAKING THE BANK AT MONTE CARLO

DECEMBER 1892: BREAKING ROCKS AT MONTE CARLO

Fair play

So much for the evils of gambling, but there are lots of ways of playing chance games that won't do you any harm at all. After all, any game with a die such as Ludo or Snakes and Ladders is a game of chance, and playing them will never hurt you – unless you happen to be on a Mississippi steamer playing Snakes and Ladders with Riverboat Lil and Brett Shuffler.

It's amazing how a few live swamp adders can sharpen your concentration, isn't it? Still, as we'd hate to lose you before we've got to the end of the book, we'll hurry home and try a few games out on Binky instead.

You and Binky each need a pile of counters but if you haven't got any, there's loads of other things you can use such as dead matchsticks or dried peas or diamonds or pearls or rubies or even bits of paper cut into little squares.

The simple coin

Take turns to toss a coin.

- If it comes down heads, Binky gives you a counter.
- If it comes down tails, you give Binky a counter.

This is a perfectly fair game, because when you toss the coin there are two possible outcomes – heads or tails – and they are both equally likely. The chance of you winning is 1 in 2. Even if you play this game for a long time, you should both finish with about the same number of counters that you started with. There's just one tiny problem...

The (slightly more exciting) die

Binky keeps throwing the die.

- Every time Binky throws a "6" you give him ONE counter.
- Every time Binky doesn't throw a "6" he gives you ONE counter.

It should be obvious to see that this game is NOT fair! In fact very soon Binky will have given you all his counters and might have got a bit upset, too. The reason is that there are six possible outcomes, because the die can land on 1, 2, 3, 4, 5 or 6, so the chances of Binky winning are only 1 in 6. To help us make things fair, let's use a slightly different way of describing the chances involved:

ODDS In this game you might say "the odds are 5 to 1 *against* Binky winning". When you talk about odds, you count up the chances of winning and the chances of not winning and you put the bigger number first. As there are 5 chances he won't win and 1 chance that he will, that makes odds of 5 to 1. The word "against" then tells us that Binky is more likely to lose than win.

If Binky's odds of winning are 5 to 1 against, what are *your* odds? When Binky throws the die, you have 5 chances of winning and 1 of losing. Again the odds of winning are 5 to 1 (always put the bigger number first) but instead of "against" we indicate that you are more likely to win by saying "the odds are 5 to 1 *on* you winning".

Let's hear it from the experts:

'ODDS AGAINST' MEANS WHATEVER YOU'RE DESCRIBING IS **NOT** LIKELY TO HAPPEN

'ODDS ON' MEANS WHATEVER YOU'RE DESCRIBING **IS** LIKELY TO HAPPEN

By the way, when you were just tossing the coin, you had 1 chance of winning and 1 of losing. If the chances are the same you don't say the odds are "1 to 1 on" or "1 to 1 against", you just say "the odds are *evens*".

Describing the chances as "odds of 5 to 1" indicates how to make the game fair. As Binky is going to lose five times for every win, when he does win you should give him five times as much. Here are the fair rules of the game:

● Every time he throws a "6" you give Binky FIVE counters.
● Every time he doesn't throw a "6" Binky gives you ONE counter.

If you play this version of the game a lot of times, you should find that you both end up with about the same number of counters that you started with.

Oh no, it's our old enemy Professor Fiendish. Trust him to sneak in and start cheating at games!

Let's see why Binky lost so quickly. Each time the professor throws, there are three possible outcomes:

The professor tosses heads first time. Binky gives him ONE counter.

The professor tosses tails the first time, but then tosses heads on his second attempt. Binky gives him ONE counter.

The professor tosses tails both times. He gives Binky TWO counters.

It seems fair enough, doesn't it? After all, there are three outcomes, and as two of them let the professor win, the chances (or "odds") seem to be 2 to 1 in his favour. That's why he gives Binky two counters when he loses. So what's the trick?

The secret is that although there are three outcomes, not all the outcomes are equally likely! This is where the tree diagram is really useful:

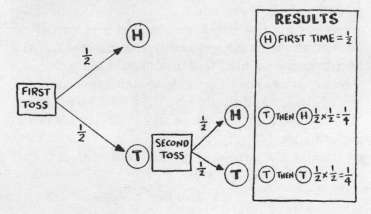

When the professor first tosses a coin, there's $\frac{1}{2}$ a chance it will come down heads and he will win straight away. There's also $\frac{1}{2}$ a chance that he will get tails first time, so he tosses again. This appears as a second event on the diagram with a pair of branches to show what could happen with his second toss – he has $\frac{1}{2}$ a chance of heads and $\frac{1}{2}$ a chance of tails.

You can calculate the chance of each outcome on the right-hand side:

● Start on the left and work along the lines to the final outcome you want to calculate.

● Write down all the fractions you pass on the way.

● MULTIPLY the fractions together to get the chance.

For example, if you want to know the chance of throwing tails then tails again, you pass $\frac{1}{2}$ and then you pass another $\frac{1}{2}$. To multiply fractions you just times the tops together and then times the bottoms. You get $\frac{1}{2} \times \frac{1}{2} = \frac{1 \times 1}{2 \times 2} = \frac{1}{4}$.

So the tree diagram not only shows how many possible outcomes there are, it also shows you how to work out the chances of each one. Best of all, you'll find that if you add up the chances of all three outcomes for the game you get $\frac{1}{2} + \frac{1}{4} + \frac{1}{4} = 1$. (Even when tree diagrams get really complicated, all the final outcomes added together should make 1.)

Now you can see that the three outcomes are NOT equally likely and that's why the professor's game is unfair. In fact, let's suppose the professor plays the game 4 times:

● 2 times the professor should win with his first toss. (Because $4 \times \frac{1}{2} = 2$)

- 1 time he should get tails with his first toss then heads with his second toss. (Because $4 \times \frac{1}{4} = 1$)
- 1 time he should get tails with both tosses. (Because $4 \times \frac{1}{4} = 1$ again.)

As you can see, the professor should win 3 times out of 4 so his chance of winning is $\frac{3}{4}$. He'll lose 1 time out of 4 so his chance of losing is $\frac{1}{4}$.

To make the game fair, remember that the professor should win 3 times for every 1 time he loses, so his chances of winning are 3 to 1. This means that when he loses he should give Binky THREE counters – not two!

Heads or dishes?

When we toss a coin, we've no idea how it will land, all we do know is that there is an equal chance of it being heads or tails. Therefore, if you toss one coin ten times you could expect the coin to come down five times on heads and five times on tails. But many people have let this information confuse them...

City: **Chicago, Illinois, U.S.A.**
Place: **Luigi's Diner**
Date: **13 February, 1929**
Time: **2.23 a.m.**

"Hey, Luigi!" called the large man as he licked the last blob of spaghetti sauce off his plate. "That was real good, just like what mamma used to make only smaller. You got any more?"

"Sorry, Mr Boccelli," replied the man standing by the cash till. "You and your associates just ate up every last item of food in the place."

"C'mon, Porky," said the shady man. "It's time we made for home. You too, Jimmy."

The three Boccelli brothers rose to their feet.

"We better be cutting along too," said the man with the crooked mouth. "I need my beauty sleep."

There was a low murmur of amusement from the others. Half-smile Gabrianni could sleep for a year and still his own mother would scribble over his face in family photographs.

Luigi snapped his fingers. "Benni!" he called. "Fetch the gentlemen's coats."

As Benni the waiter hurried through to the back room Luigi anxiously held his breath. Everything seemed calm as the seven men approached the counter.

"You done the place up nice since we last came," said the Weasel. "What d'ya say, Blade?"

"Yeah, real nice," said Blade Boccelli.

"I'm sure relieved to see your two families all getting along," said Luigi. "It's a whole lot better than having the place broken up."

The seven men looked sheepish as they recalled their last visit. The meal had been fine and friendly but dividing up the bill had been a different matter. The resulting fight had put Luigi out of business for months and they had all landed in jail.

"So how much do we owe?" asked Chainsaw Charlie.

Luigi glanced down at the bill. This was the moment that he had dreaded.

"It's, er … it comes to…" but then his nerve failed him. He tossed the slip of paper away. "Let's say it's on the house. My treat."

"Relax Luigi!" chuckled Blade, picking the bill up from the floor. "We ain't going to bust the place up! As you know, none of us is carrying any hardware. We made you a promise."

"Besides," said Weasel, "me and Blade have discussed a system to decide which family pays."

"Have you?" asked Chainsaw and Half-smile together.

"Yeah," said Blade. "We toss a coin. If you Gabriannis win, then me and Jimmy and Porky pay it all."

"And if we lose then the four of us pay the whole thing," said the Weasel.

"Weasel, we got to talk!" said Chainsaw Charlie, pulling him aside.

"Too right we do!" said Half-smile. "Will you excuse us one moment, Blade?"

The four Gabriannis put their heads together.

"What gives with you guys?" asked Weasel.

"You fool!" snapped Half-smile. "Did you see how much Porky Boccelli put away?"

"Yeah," said Chainsaw. "We can hardly pay for ourselves, never mind the guzzle monster!"

"And you know what happens if anyone can't pay their bill," moaned Half-smile. "We'll be washing Luigi's dishes for months!"

"Relax!" said Weasel. "I've been studying the laws of probability. The only money we need is one little coin and Numbers is going to sort that out right now! Get to it, Numbers."

The thin man slipped away.

In the back room Benni had put his arms around the pile of coats and with a huge effort he managed to lift all seven at once. He strained as he moved round towards the door, but the weight was too much. He fell backwards and was pinned down by a mountain of bulky material.

"Boy, I must be getting feeble," he muttered to himself, unaware that as well as the coats he had been trying to carry enough hidden rifles, handguns, bullets, grenades and coshes to wipe out a star system. Just as he was about to struggle out from under the pile he heard footsteps sneak into the room. Benni's survival instinct told him to keep very still and listen.

Ping!

"One head," muttered a voice.

Ping!

"Two heads."

Ping!

"One tail."

Benni peered out from under the pile and was amazed to see the thin man earnestly tossing a coin. After a few more tosses he seemed satisfied.

"Four heads and five tails," he announced to himself. "That's it!"

Holding the coin carefully, the thin man went back and joined the other three Gabriannis.

"You got the coin?" asked Weasel.

"It's all figured," said Numbers.

"What's figured?" asked Half-smile.

"Listen," explained Weasel. "You toss a coin, half the time it's heads, half the time it's tails, right?"

"Guess so," said Half-smile.

"So if you toss it ten times, you get five heads and five tails, uh?"

"That follows," said Chainsaw.

"I just tossed it nine times," said Numbers. "So far, five tails and four heads."

"The next toss has to be heads!" says Weasel.

"Wow!" said Chainsaw and Half-smile.

"C'mon you guys," One Finger Jimmy called over. "What are you up to?"

"Just getting a coin," said Weasel.

"Oh yeah?" asked Blade. "Well I want to see that coin."

Blade took the coin and turned it over. Sure enough it had one side heads and one side tails.

"Is it OK?" asked Porky.

"Seems fine to me!" said Blade.

"So if it falls heads you pay, and if it's tails then we pay," said Weasel.

"You guys seem pretty sure on heads turning up," said Jimmy.

48

Weasel, Chainsaw and Numbers looked at each other and suppressed a fit of giggles. Even Half-smile tried to pull a straight face which made him look even spookier than normal. "Pass the coin to Numbers," said Weasel. "He'll toss it."

"Oh no you don't," said One Finger Jimmy. "I don't know what stunt you guys are trying to pull, so I'll toss the coin."

"With one finger?" sniggered Weasel.

"That does it!" snapped Jimmy pulling something from inside his jacket. Weasel saw the glint of metal in Jimmy's hand and dived under the table.

"Er, Jimmy," said Porky. "How come you're going to shoot Weasel with your fountain pen?"

"Oh rats," said Jimmy realizing his mistake. "I forgot we didn't have our weapons. Sorry Weasel."

49

"I should think so," said Weasel, crawling out between the chair legs. "Next time show some respect and pull a gun. Bloodstains are fine, but an ink blot could ruin my good reputation."

"Let's get this thing sorted," said Blade, passing the coin to Luigi. "Would you do the honours, friend?"

"He's passed it to Luigi!" gasped Half-smile.

"Is this still going to work?" whispered Chainsaw to Weasel.

"It's still the same coin so it can't fail!" said Weasel. "Come on Luigi, let's see some action!"

Luigi tossed the coin and let it fall to the floor. The seven men eagerly leant over to look at it and all their heads collided at once with a solid CLUNK.

There were four gasps and three sniggers. The seven men stood upright again.

"Goodnight guys," said Blade taking his coat from Benni. "And many thanks."

"But … but … but…" started Chainsaw, but Blade had whipped his three-barrelled Pedley Liquidator from his coat pocket. "What was that you were saying

50

about reputation? You want a good reputation, you pay the bill like nice boys."

"Thanks fellas," said Porky. "Hey Jimmy, give me a push through this door, will you? It seems to have shrunk some."

With a heave, a creak and a slam the Boccellis were gone.

"So, gentlemen," said Luigi. "How'd you like to pay? Cash or cheque?"

"Dishcloth," they all replied as they sadly trooped through to the kitchen sink.

So what went wrong? Weasel and his friends made THREE massive mistakes...

Weasel's first mistake: A coin has no memory!

The best way to understand this is with an even sillier example. Suppose you have two identical coins and you toss one 99 times and every time it comes down heads.

Here's the big question: the next time you toss it, is it more likely to fall heads or tails? After 99 heads, you may well think that tails is almost bound to turn up because it isn't very likely that a coin will fall heads 100 times in a row, is it?

Just as you're thinking about this, three demented gerbils leap on to the table.

The answer is that neither of them is more likely. They are just coins, and the one that has fallen heads 99 times can't remember doing it! The 100th throw is just as likely to be heads as it is tails.

The coin that Numbers was tossing couldn't remember that it had just given 5 tails and 4 heads. Even if it could, how was it supposed to make sure it landed on heads? Could it grow wings and steer itself down as it landed? Or maybe it has little legs so that it could flip itself over at the last minute? Sadly not, but you'd be surprised at how many people think that coins DO have a memory. It's great fun asking people "If a coin lands 99 times on heads, are you more likely to get heads or tails on the 100th toss?" If they say "It's bound to be tails" then you can give them the little lecture about coins with wings and little legs and make them feel all silly. Ho ho, what fun.

Weasel's second mistake: Don't confuse predictions with results

When we work out the odds in a game of chance, don't forget it is a game of chance! All we are doing is deciding what the *most likely* outcome will be, but this can be very different from the actual results.

If you only play a game once or twice, then the results might be very different from your predictions. However if you play lots of times, you should find that things "average out" and overall you get what you expected.

We're about to experiment with ten coin tosses, but instead of tossing one coin ten times, we'll toss ten coins at once. In this case it will give us exactly the same results but it's a lot faster. We're going to see how many heads we can get and as the chance of each coin landing on heads is $\frac{1}{2}$ our ten coins should give us 5 heads and 5 tails. Let's see what happens...

Good grief! We only got 3 heads out of ten coins which means our success rate was $\frac{3}{10}$. Yuk, another fraction! And how does this compare with the $\frac{1}{2}$ we should expect? Let's dig up an ancient maths secret to help us.

How to COMPARE ye NASTY FRACTIONS

The favoured method is to turn each fraction into a PERCENTAGE.

Step 1: Multiply the top of ye fraction by 100.
Step 2: Divide ye answer by the bottom bit.
Step 3: Write the special % sign at the end.

And thus you have a percentage. God save the King.

This isn't too bad so let's try it on our $\frac{1}{2}$ and our $\frac{3}{10}$:

- Our expected chance was $\frac{1}{2}$ so this makes:
  $$\frac{1}{2} \times 100 = \frac{1 \times 100}{2} = \frac{100}{2} = 50\%$$

● Our experiment gave us $\frac{3}{10}$ which makes:
$\frac{3}{10} \times 100 = \frac{3 \times 100}{10} = \frac{300}{10} = 30\%$

Now it's easier to compare the results, and obviously 30% is quite a lot less than 50% so it turned out rather worse than we expected. You might say we've been unlucky to get so few heads. However, we're tough Murderous Maths types and not easily beaten, therefore we'll continue to play and keep track of our results after each toss of 10 coins. This is how the results might appear:

Toss of ten coins	Heads	% for this toss	Total Heads so far	Total coins tossed so far	Total result	Total %
1st	3	30%	3	10	3/10	30%
2nd	5	50%	8	20	8/20	40%
3rd	8	80%	16	30	16/30	53.33%
4th	2	20%	18	40	18/40	45%
5th	6	60%	24	50	24/50	48%
6th	4	40%	28	60	28/60	46.67%
7th	9	90%	37	70	37/70	52.86%
8th	5	50%	42	80	42/80	52.5%

The top line of this table shows what happened with our first toss of 10 coins – we got 3 heads and a 30% result. The second line showed what happened with the next toss – we got 5 heads which gave us a 50% result. It then shows us how many heads we'd had so far in rounds 1 and 2 which was $3 + 5 = 8$. It also shows how many tosses we'd had so far which was 20, and then the total result and finally this fraction is converted into a percentage.

You'll see that as well as our bad luck with toss 1 we also had very bad luck with toss 4. Never mind because toss 3 was a lot better and toss 7 was amazing! The main thing to notice is the total percentage at the end. After a few rounds it gets close to 50% and even after our fluke result in round 7, it still stays close to 50%.

So far we've convinced ourselves that 50% of the time a coin lands on heads, but where does that leave Weasel? If you look at our results – out of 8 throws only TWO of them happened to give 5 heads and 5 tails!

TEST HOW STRANGE YOUR LUCK IS

Why not see if you can beat the odds? Make a table like the one above with columns for you to write results in. Get 10 coins, shake them all up then drop them all on the table. Count up the heads and start filling your table in. You should find that the more lines you fill in, the closer the total percentage gets to 50%. If your percentage after 10 tosses is more than 60% or less than 40%, then you have had a very strange run of luck indeed!

Weasel's third mistake: Expecting to get 5 heads and 5 tails

Read the following statement carefully:

The most likely result from tossing a coin ten times is 5 heads and 5 tails.

This is absolutely true, but it is also one of the most fabulously misleading things you'll ever read. Check it again and see if you can spot the catch!

Now let's alter the words a bit to make it clearer:

Of all the results you can get from ten tosses, the one that is most likely to occur is 5 heads and 5 tails.

Just for a change, we'll give coins a rest and look in Pongo McWhiffy's vest drawer. Gas mask in place? Rubber gloves on? Here we go then...

Pongo has 5 vests. One has a curry stain, one was splatted by a pigeon, one has a fried egg stuck to it and two of them are slowly dying of old age. If you shut your eyes and pull out a vest, what sort of disgusting feature is it most likely to have? Here are the chances: Old age $=\frac{2}{5}$, Curry stain $=\frac{1}{5}$, Pigeon splat $=\frac{1}{5}$, Fried egg $=\frac{1}{5}$.

Now let's make a misleading statement:

The most likely feature you will find on the vest you choose is old age.

This is true because, for instance, you are twice as likely to get an old smelly vest as you are to get the one with the curry stain. In the same way, when you toss a coin ten times you are more likely to get five heads and five tails than six heads and four tails.

BUT ... although old age is the most likely disgusting vest feature, you only have a $\frac{2}{5}$ chance of getting it! As the chances of getting one of the other vests add up to $\frac{3}{5}$ it is more likely that you *won't* get one of the old ones!

This is also the case with tossing ten coins – you are actually more likely *not* to get 5 heads and 5 tails!

Well, you'd been lucky up until the tenth toss. You had 4 heads and 5 tails. The chances of the last toss landing on heads and letting you win was $\frac{1}{2}$.

Yes, they could have been.

The answer to that is 24·61% which is slightly less than $\frac{1}{4}$.

By the way, are you wondering where the figure of 24·61% comes from? Of course you are, that's why you've joined us in a Murderous Maths book. As Weasel has absolutely no chance of understanding it, we'll leave him behind as we zoom into the next chapter where we'll get the answer after we've met one of the most gorgeous things in maths.

One of the most gorgeous things in maths

Stand back, dim the lights, open the curtains, cue drum roll and...

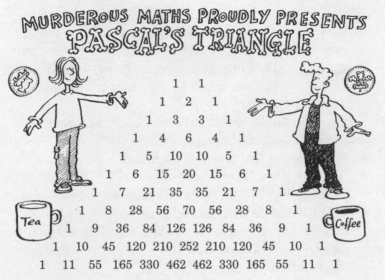

MURDEROUS MATHS PROUDLY PRESENTS
PASCAL'S TRIANGLE

```
                    1    1
                 1    2    1
              1    3    3    1
           1    4    6    4    1
        1    5   10   10    5    1
      1    6   15   20   15    6    1
    1    7   21   35   35   21    7    1
   1    8   28   56   70   56   28    8    1
 1    9   36   84  126  126   84   36    9    1
1   10   45  120  210  252  210  120   45   10    1
1   11   55  165  330  462  462  330  165   55   11    1
```

Blaise Pascal 1623–1662 – French, mathematician, religious, brilliant brain but a really irritating person, invented an early calculator, died of an agonizing illness aged 39.

That's him sorted out so now let's check his triangle. But before we do, here's a suggestion: make this page easy to find by folding over the top corner. Go on, do it, because once you've found out how brilliant Pascal's Triangle is, you'll be coming back to look at it loads of times.

How to draw your own Pascal's triangle

Although this arrangement of numbers can solve a whole ton of murderous problems, it's utterly simple to draw. All you do is make two sloping sides out of 1s then start at the top and fill in the gaps. Each number in the triangle comes from adding together the two numbers above it, so the 2 in the second row comes from adding together the two 1s. Looking further down, you'll see the 56s come from adding together the 21 and 35 above them and so on. The triangle shown here has eleven rows, but if you draw out your own triangle you can go on adding extra rows for ever.

The questions that this triangle answers are awesome. Look at these beauties:

- What is the 5th triangle number?
- What is the x^4 coefficient of $(1+x)^8$?
- What is the 7th tetrahedral number?
- What is the 6th Fibonacci number?

Wahey! Actually you probably won't understand any of that lot unless you have an especially huge mathsy head like this:

COR! PASCAL'S TRIANGLE! SLOBBER! DROOL!

As far as us normal-headed people are concerned, the best thing about Pascal's triangle is that it gives us a completely wicked short cut to finding out what happens when we toss coins up. Thank goodness, because if we had to do the sums involved, we'd need heads the size of armchairs.

AND EVEN MEGA-BRAINY MATHS BODS LIKE A SHORT CUT SOME OF THE TIME!

Speaking of heads, you'll notice that there is a picture of a "head" and a "tail" either side of the triangle to help explain what's going on.

One coin

Look at the top line, all you can see are two 1s. This line tells you what can happen if you toss up one coin. *If you add up the numbers on the line it tells you how many possible outcomes there are.* Stand by for a tough sum: $1 + 1 = 2$. (You can check this on your calculator if you like.) This means there are two outcomes from tossing one coin. Of course we knew that because you can either get one head or one tail. The top line also tells us about the one head and one tail because there is a "1" on the heads side and a "1" on the tails side. Isn't that pretty?

Don't worry if you're feeling confused, it's probably because this is all *too* simple. Let's move on.

Two coins

The second line (1-2-1) tells us what can happen when you toss two coins. If we add up the numbers it tells us that there are 4 possible outcomes. To see what these outcomes are, we'll draw them out and it helps to understand what's going on if we use two different coins, say 1p and 2p:

Sure enough, those are all the different ways that two coins can fall and they are both heads OR both tails OR 1p heads, 2p tails OR 1p tails, 2p heads.

The lovely thing about "1-2-1" is that it tells us about these different outcomes without us having to draw them out:

- The "1" at the heads side tells us there is only ONE way of getting both coins as heads. (We'll call this HH from now on to make it neater.)
- The "2" in the middle tells us that there are TWO ways of getting one head and one tail. (These are HT or TH.)
- The "1" at the tails side tells us there is only ONE way of getting both coins as tails. (We'll call this TT.)

From this we can work out the chances of getting the different outcomes:

HH	1 chance in 4	or $\frac{1}{4}$
HT or TH	2 chances in 4	or $\frac{2}{4}$
TT	1 chance in 4	or $\frac{1}{4}$

Remember that all the chances of all the different outcomes must add up to 1, so let's try it:

$\frac{1}{4} + \frac{2}{4} + \frac{1}{4} = \frac{4}{4} = 1$. Yes indeed! How super. We can even check this on a tree diagram:

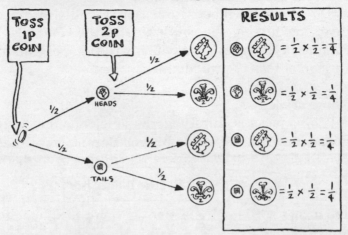

First of all we imagine we've tossed the 1p coin and get either heads or tails. Then we imagine we toss the 2p coin and and see what we get. The four possible outcomes are shown at the end, and they all have a chance of $\frac{1}{4}$.

The four different outcomes are obvious if the coins are different, but the hard bit to realize is that if the coins are identical there are still four different outcomes. What confuses things is that with identical coins, two of the outcomes look the same. HT looks just like TH so it *seems* like you can only get three outcomes: both heads, both tails or one of each.

This gives the impression that the chances of each outcome are $\frac{1}{3}$ or 33%. WRONG!

(Do you remember Professor Fiendish's trick involving tossing the coin twice in the "Fair play" chapter? That trick is a devilishly cunning disguised version of tossing two identical coins.)

Three drinks

All this maths is thirsty work, so let's go and visit Pongo McWhiffy's Deluxe Burger Bar.

Pongo has two brown liquids on sale and he claims that one is tea and the other is coffee. Three bus drivers call by every morning and each driver picks one of the brown liquids at random. As there's an equal chance of it being either tea or coffee, this is like tossing a coin. The chance of tea is $\frac{1}{2}$ and the chance of coffee is also $\frac{1}{2}$.

What are the chances that Pongo served up three teas this morning?

As 3 drinks are involved, we look at the third line of the triangle and find 1-3-3-1. This tells us that there are:

1 OUTCOME WITH 3 TEAS AND 0 COFFEE	3 OUTCOMES WITH 2 TEAS AND 1 COFFEE	3 OUTCOMES WITH 1 TEA AND 2 COFFEES	1 OUTCOME WITH 0 TEAS AND 3 COFFEES
(T) (T) (T)	(T) (T) (C)	(C) (C) (T)	(C) (C) (C)
	(T) (C) (T)	(T) (C) (C)	
	(C) (T) (T)	(C) (T) (C)	

You'll notice that for each number we move along the line, this represents the outcomes with one less tea and one more coffee. Every line in the triangle works like this.

If we add up $1+3+3+1$ we find there are 8 possible outcomes altogether, and only one of them has three teas. This tells us that the chance of all three drivers having tea is $\frac{1}{8}$. (Pongo's 3 mugs all look different, but even if they looked the same, there would still be 8 possible outcomes.)

SO IS THIS TEA OR COFFEE?

I THINK IT'S CHIP GREASE

MINE DOESN'T WANT TO COME OUT...

Six coins

Let's skip down a bit and see what happens on line 6: 1-6-15-20-15-6-1

If you toss up six coins you get:

- Total possible outcomes:
  $1+6+15+20+15+6+1=64$
- How many outcomes with 6H 0T?   1
- How many outcomes with 5H 1T?   6
- How many outcomes with 4H 2T?   15
- How many outcomes with 3H 3T?   20

...and so on. (6H 0T means 6 heads and 0 tails if you hadn't guessed.)

What are the chances of getting exactly 3 heads and 3 tails? Easy, there's 20 outcomes that give 3H 3T and 64 outcomes in total so the chance is $\frac{20}{64}$ which is the same as 31·25%.

Pascal's powers of two

If you multiply a row of twos by themselves you get different powers. For instance $2 \times 2 \times 2$ is "2 to the power of 3" and you can write it like this: 2^3. If you work it out you find $2 \times 2 \times 2 = 8$. Here's something spooky! If you add up the numbers on line 3 of the triangle, what do you get? $1+3+3+1=8$.

Try 2^4. If you multiply $2 \times 2 \times 2 \times 2$ you get 16. If you look at line 4 you'll see the numbers are 1-4-6-4-1. What do you get if you add them up? Go on, surprise yourself.

Yes, one of the amazing things about the triangle is that you can use it work out any power of 2 without having to multiply. For instance if you need to know 2^7 you just add up all the numbers on the 7th line. It's easy to find the 7th line because

"7" is the number next to the edge. You get $1 + 7 + 21 + 35 + 35 + 21 + 7 + 1 = 128$, which is the right answer!

People who live in shoes

You probably know the old nursery rhyme:

There was an old woman who lived in a shoe. She had so many children she didn't know what to do...

Fancy not knowing what to do! If she had any sense she'd move out of the shoe for a start. Honestly.

Just for fun, let's suppose she has nine kids. What are the chances of them being seven girls and two boys? Easy! As there are nine kids, look at line 9 which is 1-9-36-84-126-126-84-36-9-1. Add it up (or work out 2^9) and get the total outcomes: 512. Now start at the end and work along but instead of heads and tails, think about girls and boys. There's one outcome of 9 girls 0 boys, nine outcomes of 8 girls 1 boy and then we reach the one we want: 36 outcomes of 7 girls and 2 boys.

The chance of 7 girls and 2 boys works out at $\frac{36}{512}$ which comes to about 7%. Isn't that great? Even nursery rhymes aren't safe from a bit of Murderous Maths.

Ten coins

Do you remember Weasel's bet where they tossed a coin 10 times? This is the same as tossing 10 coins once so let's look at line 10 and the outcomes:

Line 10: 1   10   45   120 210 252 210 120 45   10   1
Outcome: 10H 9H 8H 7H 6H 5H 4H 3H 2H 1H 0H
         0T   1T 2T 3T 4T 5T 6T 7T 8T 9T 10T

How many possible outcomes altogether? Simple. It's 2^{10} – which you can get by adding up all the numbers on line 10 – and it comes to 1024.

How many of the possible outcomes would give 5 heads and 5 tails? Easy. It's 252. (A quick tip: whenever you have an even number of coins, the chances of half heads and half tails is always the biggest number which is in the middle of the line.)

So what was the chance of getting 5 heads and 5 tails in 10 tosses? It's $\frac{252}{1024}$ which works out as 24·61%. As we said before, it's slightly less than 25% which is $\frac{1}{4}$.

Although 5H5T is the most likely result because it has the biggest number of possible outcomes, you'll see that 6H4T has 210 outcomes and 4H6T has 210 outcomes as well. It's interesting to think about the chances of getting six coins landing the same way – in other words getting either 6 heads or 6 tails.

There are 210 outcomes of 6H4T and 210 outcomes of 4H6T. If you add those together you get 420 outcomes which have either six heads or six tails. If you work out $\frac{420}{1024}$ as a percentage (i.e. multiply it by $\frac{100}{1}$) it turns out to be more than 40%. So if you throw ten coins you are far more likely to get six coins the same than five the same! Of course, that's just as long as you aren't fussy if the six coins are all heads or all tails.

So now you're ready for anything...

You decide to grab a handful of coppers and dash off to show your best mate all about coin tossing and Pascal's Triangle. But just as you hurry down the street your eye is caught by some lights flickering from within a brightly striped tent. What is it? A circus? A fairground? It's no good, you simply have to look, so you make a detour and approach the open flap.

"Fin fir ill the fimily," comes a voice from a tinny loudspeaker. "Lits and lits iv fin."

"Fun for all the family?" you wonder as you step through the opening. Immediately behind you there is a loud CLANG. You spin round to see the tent flap has closed.

Clang? What a funny noise for a tent flap to make. But of course this is no ordinary tent flap, and indeed no ordinary tent.

"Welcome to my reinforced titanium steel tent!" chuckles a ghastly voice. "From which there is no escape!"

"Oh no!" You curse your foolishness. How could you be so silly?

"Oh yes!" replies the voice. Then with a flash and a bang your arch-enemy Professor Fiendish appears. Actually you are quite impressed.

"You don't normally appear with a flash and a bang," you remark.

"Bah," says the Fiendish One as he untangles his foot from a bundle of cables. "That's because I don't normally trip over my electric meter."

You watch amazed as blue sparks shoot up the tent poles and dance across the roof.

"Brilliant," you mutter. "You've managed to make your metal tent completely live with electricity."

"Har har!" laughs the professor. "It's all part of my cunning plan to keep you here for ever!"

As he speaks you notice he puts a 1p coin into the side of the generator.

"The meter will keep the current running just so long as I keep putting pennies into it," he sniggers. "And I've got hundreds of them, AND I'm going to get some more!"

"Where from?" you mutter.

"You!" laughs the professor, pointing at your spending money. "We're going to play a little game and soon all you have will be mine, mine ... MINE!"

You look around the tent. It seems that the professor has been trying to get some sad little amusement arcade going because you notice a little table with a sign above it.

"Fancy a flutter, do you?" asks the professor. "I knew you couldn't resist. It will cost you a penny a turn until I win all your money!"

"Sorry, but I'm not in the mood," you say as you move back towards the tent flap. But just as you approach it, a hairy blue blast of light zaps towards you. You leap aside then look down to see smoke coming from the place where you've just been standing.

There's nothing for it, so you work out your chances on the game. Line 6 of Pascal's triangle tells you that when you toss 6 coins there are 64 possible outcomes. Only one of these is all heads so your chances of winning are 1 in 64. If the professor is only paying 60p when you get all heads, out of every 64p you pay him you can only expect 60p back.

Slowly but surely, you'll lose everything! But then a bit of brilliance occurs to you...

"OK, let's play!" you announce with unnerving brightness.

The professor passes you six golden tossing coins and eyes you suspiciously. You pay a penny and throw them. Four heads and two tails.

"Har har, you lose" chuckles the professor.

"But what fun!" you answer. "Can I have another go?"

"Oh, I insist," he says as he snatches your next penny.

You toss again throwing the coins down hard on to the table with excitement. One head, five tails.

"Har har," says the professor. "You lose again."

But with a nonchalant smirk you hand over yet another penny for your next turn. You seize the tossing coins and throw them down even harder ... whoops! They fly off the table and roll all over the ground – and in the confusion the professor doesn't realize that you've sneakily shoved one of them up your sleeve. You watch as he scrabbles about on the ground.

"I'm so terribly sorry," you say. "I was having such fun too!"

"I'll find them, and then you'll keep playing again and again until you've lost everything!" he snarls.

"That sounds jolly," you say.

But after several minutes of frantic searching the professor can only find five coins.

"We'll just play with five then," you suggest, "and if I get all heads you pay me 60p."

"No!" says the professor. "That's not fair. You'll win!"

"Oh," you reply sounding disappointed. "I tell you what, as it was 60p for throwing six heads, why not give me 50p if I throw five heads?"

"Har har!" says the professor. "Now THAT sounds fair."

So on you play with the new rules and it doesn't take too long before you've cleaned the professor right out. The blue sparks stop and soon you're heading off on your way, although you can only move slowly because your pockets are exploding with mountains of the professor's money.

"Lits and lits iv fin fir ill the fimily" says the loudspeaker, but it doesn't quite disguise the sad whimpering sounds made by the professor. He's not having lits and lits iv fin and it serves him right too.

So why did you start winning?

Answer: When you toss 6 coins there are 64 possible outcomes, so your chance of winning is $\frac{1}{64}$. Even with a prize of 60p for all heads, you would slowly lose. However, when you toss 5 coins there are only 32 possible outcomes, so your chance of winning is $\frac{1}{32}$. As the professor agreed to pay 50p every time you got the five heads outcome, the chances are that for every 32p you staked, you won back 50p. No wonder it didn't take long to win all his money!

The dead simple £1,000,000 trick

If you toss three coins, line 3 of Pascal's triangle tells you that there's a $\frac{1}{8}$ chance that you'll get 3 heads and a $\frac{1}{8}$ chance you'll get 3 tails. Adding these together gives you a $\frac{2}{8}$ or 25% chance that all three coins will land the same way. But what about the chances of *at least two* coins landing the same way?

To illustrate this, we'll pop in to Fogsworth Manor and catch Rodney Bounder playing his favourite trick...

So anytime you're short of £1,000,000, that's all you need to do.

A last thought

Toss 24 coins in the air. The chance of them all landing on heads is 1 in 2^{24} which makes 1 in 16,777,216.

The chance of winning the national lottery jackpot is 1 in 13,983,816.

So winning the jackpot is easier than throwing 24 straight heads.

Perms, coms, curries, burgers, bells and the lottery

Has this happened to you yet?

OOH! YOU'RE READING A BOOK ABOUT PROBABILITY! SO AM I LIKELY TO WIN THE LOTTERY?

If not, then it will definitely happen soon. All you need to do is turn back and check the last page...

YOUR CHANCE OF WINNING THE JACKPOT IS 1 IN 13,983,816!

Hopefully you might get away with it unless this happens...

WHY?

In that case you need to say...

BECAUSE THERE ARE 49 NUMBERS TO CHOOSE FROM AND YOU CAN PICK ANY COMBINATION OF SIX OF THEM, THEREFORE THE TOTAL NUMBER OF POSSIBLE COMBINATIONS IS $\frac{49!}{43! \times 6!}$ WHICH COMES TO 13,983,816 OF WHICH ONLY ONE IS THE WINNER

That should be enough to silence them, but because you're a Murderous Maths reader, you'll be wondering what $\frac{49!}{43! \times 6!}$ means and where it comes from.

The special sign: !

Usually when you see ! in a book it means the person writing it is trying to be funny (this book's full of them) but when it comes after a number it's called a **factorial**. The exciting bit is that chance sums are about the only time it ever turns up. A factorial comes after a number like this: 7! and in this case it means $7 \times 6 \times 5 \times 4 \times 3 \times 2 \times 1$. It only works for whole numbers (you can't have $4\frac{1}{2}$!) and you have to multiply the number by all the smaller numbers right down to 1. This sign even has a nickname because if you see 12! you can call it "twelve factorial" or for short you can call it "twelve *bang*".

Here are the values of 1! to 10!

$$1! = 1 \quad 2! = 2 \quad 3! = 6 \quad 4! = 24 \quad 5! = 120 \quad 6! = 720$$

Wahey – these are starting to get big, aren't they?

$$7! = 5{,}040 \quad 8! = 40{,}320 \quad 9! = 362{,}880$$
$$10! = 3{,}628{,}800$$

And just for fun:

$$20! = 2{,}432{,}902{,}008{,}176{,}640{,}000$$

By the way, the pure mathematicians had a wonderful time deciding what $0!$ comes to. Their final conclusion was something like this:

So there you have it: $0! = 1$

By now you've worked out that the lottery chance of 1 in $\frac{49!}{43! \times 6!}$ means 1 in

$$\frac{\begin{matrix} 49 \times 48 \times 47 \times 46 \times 45 \times 44 \times 43 \times 42 \times 41 \times 40 \times 39 \times 38 \times 37 \times 36 \times 35 \times 34 \\ \times 33 \times 32 \times 31 \times 30 \times 29 \times 28 \times 27 \times 26 \times 25 \times 24 \times 23 \times 22 \times 21 \times 20 \times 19 \\ \times 18 \times 17 \times 16 \times 15 \times 14 \times 13 \times 12 \times 11 \times 10 \times 9 \times 8 \times 7 \times 6 \times 5 \times 4 \times 3 \times 2 \times 1 \end{matrix}}{\begin{matrix} 43 \times 42 \times 41 \times 40 \times 39 \times 38 \times 37 \times 36 \times 35 \times 34 \times 33 \times 32 \times 31 \times 30 \times 29 \\ \times 28 \times 27 \times 26 \times 25 \times 24 \times 23 \times 22 \times 21 \times 20 \times 19 \times 18 \times 17 \times 16 \times 15 \times 14 \\ \times 13 \times 12 \times 11 \times 10 \times 9 \times 8 \times 7 \times 6 \times 5 \times 4 \times 3 \times 2 \times 1 \end{matrix}} \times 6 \times 5 \times 4 \times 3 \times 2 \times 1$$

Be honest, don't you feel proud to be reading a book with utterly fabulous sums like this in it? All we have to do now is find out where all these numbers come from.

WARNING: If some of the next bits seem a bit tricky, that's because … they are. Don't worry if you find some of it confusing the first time you read it.

Permutations and combinations

The good news is that this gives us an excuse to visit The Ravenous Rajah, so pull up a chair, tuck in your napkin and off we go...

For £1 you get three face-firing courses. In fact the melon makes steam come out of your nose, then the curry makes steam come out of your ears and after the trifle you have to stand up to let the steam out. It's all great fun, the only snag is that there's no other choices. In terms of maths, there is only one combination of dishes that you can have and this combination includes melon, curry and trifle. Still, for £1 you could afford to go every night, couldn't you?

Now there's an idea. Instead of melon then curry then trifle you could start with the curry, then have the trifle and finish with melon. Or start with trifle, then have the curry and then melon. Or start with the melon, then have trifle and … oh, you get the general idea. The question is, in how many different orders could you eat the three dishes?

For those of us without cast-iron faces, let's think it through. In maths, different orders are called **permutations** (or "perms" for short) so what we're asking is: "If you have a combination of 3 things, how many perms are there?"

- To start with you have to decide on what to have first. You have 3 different choices which are melon, curry or trifle.

- You then select your second dish. There are two choices left so the second dish doubles the number of ways you could combine dishes in your meal. (So for example, if you started with curry, you could follow it with either melon OR trifle.) This makes the number of possible ways you could eat the first two courses: $3 \times 2 = 6$.

- When it comes to the third course you have to have the one dish left over, so there's a last choice of 1. This brings your total choices for the meal to $3 \times 2 \times 1 = 6$.

The important thing to notice here is that you only had one combination. It doesn't matter what order you eat the three dishes in, at the end of the meal there would be the same mixture of melon, curry and trifle inside your stomach. If you don't believe it then have a look…

Not a pretty sight, but at least it'll remind you that *with combinations, the order does not matter*.

So far we've worked out that if you have a combination of 3 items, there are $3 \times 2 \times 1$ permutations, and already you'll have guessed how the ! sign comes in handy. We can say that if you have 3 things, there are 3! perms. We need this result for later, so we'll mark it with a blob of curried trifle.

Phew! Anyway, rapidly moving on…

The other thing to know is that the more items you have in your combination, then the more possible permutations there are.

£1.20 FRIDAY SPECIAL MENU

STARTER: CURRIED MELON

ENTREE: CURRIED FISH FINGERS

MAIN COURSE: CURRIED CURRY

DESSERT: CURRIED TRIFLE

COFFEE: CURRIED COFFEE

On Fridays you get five dishes. If you eat them all, there is still only one combination, but there are more permutations. In fact there are $5 \times 4 \times 3 \times 2 \times 1$ perms which you can write as 5! and it comes to 120.

Up until now, making a decision about your meal has been simple. You know exactly what you're going to eat, the only question has been what order you eat it in.

Pongo's Burger Bar

Let's step outside and sample the culinary delights awaiting us at Pongo McWhiffy's Deluxe Burger Bar.

Pongo has 7 different things and you can choose any 3 of them, so how many different meals could you have?

It's easier with sums!

Let's suppose you pick the first item you want, then the second and then the third. To start with there's a choice of 7 items, then 6 then 5. This means that the total number of possible permutations of three items from a choice of seven is $7 \times 6 \times 5 = 210$. Again, using the factorial sign gives us a much neater way of writing out sums like $7 \times 6 \times 5$. Look at this:

$$\frac{7!}{4!} = \frac{7 \times 6 \times 5 \times 4 \times 3 \times 2 \times 1}{4 \times 3 \times 2 \times 1} = 7 \times 6 \times 5$$

You can see the $4 \times 3 \times 2 \times 1$ bit cancels out from top and bottom, so if you start with $\frac{7!}{4!}$ you are left with $7 \times 6 \times 5$.

The perms formula

Just imagine you're looking at a menu with 43 items on it and you're allowed to choose 9 of them.

How many different orders could you eat your 9 choices in? In other words, how many perms of 9 items from a choice of 43 are there?

This is how to work out the total number of perms for any number of items:

$$\text{Total perms} = \frac{(\text{total number of items you can choose from})!}{(\text{number of items you CAN'T choose})!}$$

To start with, imagine you could choose ALL 43 items off the menu. How many perms would there be? The number of items to choose from is 43. The number of items you can't choose is 0. So your total number of perms is $\frac{43!}{0!}$. We already know that $0! = 1$ so your number of perms would be 43!

Remember a few pages back when we had the £1 special menu? There were 3 items and we had them all. According to this formula, the number of perms is $\frac{3!}{0!}$ which comes to 3! If you look back at the bit next to the blob of curried trifle, you'll see that's the answer we got before, so it works.

Now then, suppose you can only choose 9 items from a menu of 43 different things. How many perms could you get?

Er ... the rest of us will just use the formula. Obviously there are 43 items to choose from, and the number of items you *can't* choose is $(43-9)$ which makes 34. We put these into the formula and find that there are $\frac{43!}{34!}$ perms. This works out to be more than 200,000,000,000,000 and so if Pongo served up every one, it would be enough for everybody in the world to have a different nine course meal every day for about 100 years.

Back to reality.

With Pongo's normal menu, we could choose 3 things from a list of 7, so the number of items we can't choose is 4. That's how we got the total number of perms to be $\frac{7!}{4!}$ which we've already seen makes 210.

The combinations formula

In other words there are six permutations, but just one combination. This makes sense to us. Look back again at the bit we marked with the blob of curried trifle. If we have a combination of 3 things, we can make 3! perms which is 6.

Pongo claims that one combination gives six different meals, and he says he can make 210 "different meals". Therefore the number of DIFFERENT combinations must be $210 \div 6$. That makes 35.

Let's go over this sum slowly because it's a bit tricky. There are two things to realize here:

- There are six permutations of every possible combination of three items. (For example if the combination was tomatoes, egg and sausage, this would be a different combination to the one we've just seen, and it also has six perms.)
- We have already worked out all the possible permutations of all the combinations to be 210.

So, by dividing 210 (total perms of all the combinations of 3 things we could choose) by 6 (which is how many perms of each *different* combination there are) we get the total number of different combinations. It's easy to get choked up by things such as "permutations of combinations" so let's have a quick look at something simple that has nothing to do with combinations.

Aha, perfect timing! It's the Evil Gollarks from the planet Zog.

Yeah, yeah. Anyway, Gollarks have six toes each. If there are 210 toes on board their battle cruiser, how many Gollarks are there? Answer:

$$\text{number of Gollarks} = \frac{\text{total number of toes}}{\text{number of toes on each Gollark}} = \frac{210}{6} = 35$$

The question is, will they still be calm when they realize they've shoved their spaceship control panel out of the door?

OK, let's get back to combinations where we have pretty much the same sum...

$$\frac{\text{number of combinations}}{} = \frac{\text{total number of perms}}{\text{number of perms of each combination}} = \frac{210}{6} = 35$$

That's it! If Pongo has 7 items on his menu and lets you pick 3 different ones, then there are 35 different combinations.

Congratulations! You've just got past the trickiest bit of maths in the book.

92

Now we can make things easier by getting rid of perms from this formula. If we look at the same sum written out with factorials, something rather groovy turns up:

- Each combination of 3 things has 3! perms. (This makes 6.)
- We know that the total possible number of perms is $\frac{7!}{4!}$ (Which is 210.)

So to get the number of different combinations when we choose 3 items from a total of 7 (which, incidentally, you can write as $^7C_3$) we divide the $\frac{7!}{4!}$ by 3! The sum looks like this: $^7C_3 = \frac{7!}{4! \times 3!}$

You'll see the numbers on the bottom add up to the number on the top, i.e. $4 + 3 = 7$. This is no coincidence! In fact the combinations formula for any number of items is...

$$\text{number of combinations} = \frac{(\text{total number of items you can choose from}) !}{(\text{items you can choose}) ! \times (\text{items you can't choose})!}$$

- Remember: for the combinations formula the two numbers on the bottom always add up to the number on the top.

And now ... the lottery!

For anyone doing the UK lottery, there are 49 numbers to choose from and they can choose 6 of them. This means there are 43 numbers that they can't choose. How many possible combinations does this make?

$$\text{number of lottery combinations} = {}^{49}C_6 = \frac{49!}{6! \times 43!} = 13{,}983{,}816$$

And that's how this chapter started!

By the way, here we've only worked out the chances of the lottery jackpot. You can also use combination formulas to work out the chances of the other prizes, but it all starts to get a bit fiddly so we'll move on to something else. (How to work out the other lottery chances is just one of the amazing features you'll find at: www.murderousmaths.co.uk)

The disappearing sum

It's Friday evening. The lovely Veronica Gumfloss has been out with the football team who have all escorted her safely back to her doorstep. It's that tender moment when each hopeful player closes his eyes and leans forward with quivering lips. Unfortunately Veronica's parents heard them clumping down the road and Veronica knows she only has time to kiss four out of the eleven of them if she's going to do it properly.

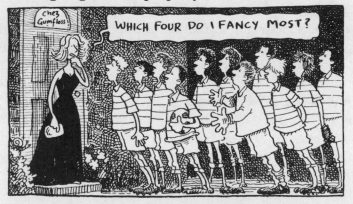

How many choices has she got? It's $^{11}C_4$ which is $\frac{11!}{4! \times 7!}$ but for goodness sake DON'T reach for the calculator! The most brilliant thing about perms and coms is that the answer can never be a fraction which means that EVERYTHING ON THE BOTTOM ALWAYS CANCELS OUT! It's probably the best fun you'll ever have with a pencil so here we go...

$$\frac{11!}{4! \times 7!} = \frac{11 \times 10 \times 9 \times 8 \times 7 \times 6 \times 5 \times 4 \times 3 \times 2 \times 1}{4 \times 3 \times 2 \times 1 \ \times \ 7 \times 6 \times 5 \times 4 \times 3 \times 2 \times 1}$$

(Before we continue, grab this book and show somebody this sum. Rub their face on it if you need to and tell them that this is the sort of thing you do for fun without a calculator these days because you're so brilliant.)

Off we go then. For starters we'll get rid of the 7! bit from top and bottom and get:

$$\frac{11 \times 10 \times 9 \times 8}{4 \times 3 \times 2 \times 1}$$

Pow! That's already got rid of more than half the numbers. Next we'll see that the 4×2 on the bottom cancels out the 8 on top (and we don't need that "$\times 1$" on the bottom either). We're left with...

$$\frac{11 \times 10 \times 9}{3}$$

Then the 3 on the bottom divides into the 9 on top leaving it as a 3 so all we've got now is:

$$\text{Veronica's choices} = 11 \times 10 \times 3$$

Look! No bottom.

If you want to use your calculator now then get on with it. You'll find that Veronica has 330 kissing combos to choose from. That's a different combination for every Friday night for the next $6\frac{1}{3}$ years!

Of course you could have used a calculator for the whole sum…

You see? Calculators can be really naff when you know how to use your brains. Can you imagine being told to write a 20-page history essay, but then you suddenly see a short cut and you only end up having to write a page and half? Of course this never happens with history, or any other subject for that matter, but when you are working out perms and coms, this happens all the time. Massive sums collapse to bits before your eyes and … oooh, it feels good. And now that we know what we are doing, it's about to feel even better!

Now for the BRILLIANT news…

Would you believe there is an EVEN SHORTER SHORT CUT to working out combinations?

Remember when we chose three out of the seven items on Pongo's menu and we found there were 35 possible combinations? We've had the number 35 elsewhere in this book. Can you think where?

ERM... ON THE BOTTOM OF PAGE 35?

SCREAM. Oh all right, yes, of course it's there, but the number 35 also appears somewhere far more gorgeous. Here are some more clues:

Suppose we were allowed to choose ONE of the seven items. How many different combinations would we be able to have? It's hardly worth working out because the answer is obviously seven.

Suppose we could choose TWO of the seven items. How many combinations could we have? The sum would look like this:

$$\frac{7!}{5! \times 2!} = \frac{7 \times 6 \times 5 \times 4 \times 3 \times 2 \times 1}{5 \times 4 \times 3 \times 2 \times 1 \ \times \ 2 \times 1} = \frac{42}{2} = 21$$

With the THREE courses the sum worked out to be

$$\frac{7!}{4! \times 3!} = 35$$

If we chose FOUR courses we'd get almost the same sum and exactly the same answer:

$$\frac{7!}{3! \times 4!} = 35$$

We won't go any further for now, but just look at that sequence of numbers. 7-21-35-35. Does it ring a bell? It might help if you wonder how many combinations you have with NO items. The answer is that there is only 1 way of having an empty plate! So our sequence is now 1-7-21-35-35

Yes yes yes! Turn back to the page with the corner that you folded over, and there it is! If you can choose from seven items, line 7 of Pascal's triangle tells you the combinations you can have. You start at one side and count along *starting with zero*.

How thrilling. Choosing from eight items means we look at line 8 of the triangle which goes like this: 1-8-28-56-70-56-28-8-1

If we are allowed five items from a choice of 8, how many combinations does this give us? Count along 0,1,2,3,4,5 and we get 56 possible combinations! You can check it with the combinations formula: $^8C_5 = \frac{8}{5! \times 3!}$. Have a go at working it out: what do you get?

This even works when we are sorting out Veronica's boyfriends. Look at line 11, and count along 0,1,2,3,4 … what do you find?

REAL heavy metal music

If you've ever fancied making some seriously loud music, then see how this appeals to you…

● Making music that can be heard from miles away.
● Nobody can tell you to be quiet.
● It's completely tuneless!
● You might even make some pocket money from it.
The answer is to find a church or hall or other building with a bell tower and go bell-ringing. There are thousands of working bell towers all over the British Isles and many other parts of the world too. The best bit is that the bells are usually very heavy – often half a tonne or more – and *very* loud. Once you've picked up the knack of getting a huge bell swinging and controlling it by pulling on a rope then you've got some serious fun coming your way.

Usually a tower will only have about 6 bells in it and each one makes a different note – it's a bit like having six different notes on a piano. Each of the bells needs one person to work it and whenever they start playing they are rung in the order 1-2-3-4-5-6. Bell number 1 is the "treble" which means it makes the highest note and it is usually the smallest bell. Bell number 6 is the "tenor" and makes the lowest note.

The fun part is that you can't play even simple tunes because the bells are so heavy. Once they are swinging you can only speed them up or slow them down very slightly to change the order in which they ring. Suppose a band of ringers tried to play "Jingle Bells", the bells would probably need to ring in this order: 4-4-4-4-4-4-4-2-6-5-4. The person ringing bell number 4 would end up looking like this:

By the way, don't let the vicar catch you hanging around like this or you'll be tolled off. (In case you didn't realize, that was a bell-ringer joke.)

So what's this got to do with maths? The answer is that as you can't play tunes, instead you ring *permutations*. As the permutations keep changing, bell-ringers call them "changes". These changes have to follow strict rules called "methods" and the pile of numbers coming up next show all the changes in a simple method called *Plain Hunt Minor*:

123456
214365
241635
426153
462513
645231
654321
563412
536142
351624
315264
132546
123456

The method starts with 1-2-3-4-5-6, then when everybody has had a BONG the order changes to 2-1-4-3-6-5, and then it changes to 2-4-1-6-3-5 and so on. You'll see that every line has a different permutation of the six bells until they come back round to 1-2-3-4-5-6 again.

To stop anybody having to speed up or slow down too much, a bell can only swap places with the bell in front or behind it each time. You can see this if you draw a line through all the "1"s – it runs in smooth diagonals down the page, it never skips from the front of the line to the back. It's the same for all the other numbers.

As *Plain Hunt* is rather simple and there are lots of permutations that don't get included (e.g. 1-5-3-4-2-6 or 6-2-3-4-5-1) over the centuries bell-ringers have invented hundreds of more mind-boggling methods. These include extra variations called "bobs" and "singles" which mean that a good band of ringers can get through all the possible permutations before they get back to 1-2-3-4-5-6 again.

So if you've got six bells, how many different permutations are there? Simple – there are 6! which makes 720. (*Plain Hunt Minor* only included 12 of these.) If you rang a clever method which worked through all the permutations it would take about 25 minutes. It starts with 1-2-3-4-5-6 but by the time a few minutes have passed the sound is fabulously confusing. However (if you get it right) suddenly like magic it comes out at the end with 1-2-3-4-5-6 again. Once you've managed this a few times, it's completely addictive! What's even better is that if you get this good, you might be asked to ring the bells for weddings or christenings which usually means being paid.

PRICE LIST
TINKLE — 10P
JINGLE — 15P
BING — 25P
BONG — 50P
DANNG — 75P
KA-DONNNG £1

Peals and quarters

On special occasions really good bell-ringers ring a "peal". It doesn't matter how many bells you have, you have to ring 5,040 changes. This means with six bells, you need to go through every permutation seven times and it would take about three hours.

A "quarter" peal is a lot easier on the arms, because you only have to ring 1,260 changes which should take about 45 minutes.

Big towers

Some towers have fewer than six bells, but many have a lot more.

- If you've got 8 bells then there are 8! possible changes which comes to 40,320. If you wanted to ring through them all then you'd be going non-stop for about 24 hours.
- With 10 bells there are 10! changes which would take about three months of non-stop ringing.

- There are about 100 towers with 12 bells in the world, and to ring all the 12! changes would take about 33 *years*.

This is building up to be bad news for the ringers at St Martin's Parish Church in Birmingham. They have an awesome 16 bells and the biggest weighs nearly two tonnes! If they wanted to ring all their 16! possible combinations, they would need to keep going non-stop for about *1·5 million years*. In this time each bell, including the two-tonne monster, would have chimed over *20 million million* times.

Dice, dates and devious decks

Earlier in the book we saw that coins have no memory.

It turns out that dice are no better.

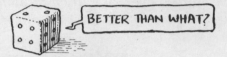

But if you've got a pack of cards, sometimes they can remember what has happened.

Oh all right, cards haven't actually got brains and nerves and grey squidgy stuff, but this demonstration will show you what's going on:

To start with, give the die a throw. What do you get?

Fair enough. The die had six sides and there was a $\frac{1}{6}$ chance of getting a two and you got it. Now if you throw the die again, could you get another two?

That's right because the die hasn't changed. It still has a two on it so if you throw it again, it still has a $\frac{1}{6}$ chance of giving you another 2. Because the first throw doesn't affect the second throw, these outcomes are called **independent**.

Now let's try the six cards. Shuffle them up and then turn the top one over.

Just like the die, there were six numbers you could have got. Your chance of getting the three was $\frac{1}{6}$. Now leave the three to one side and turn over the next card. Could it be the three again?

In this case the outcomes are *not* independent. The first card you picked HAS affected what the second card will be because the second card has to be different. If you like, the cards can "remember" what you've already picked and won't let you pick it again. When outcomes have to be different, they are called **mutually exclusive**. (In case a little bell is pinging in your head – you're right! We already came across mutually exclusive outcomes on page 21.)

It's important to know when things are independent or mutually exclusive because it makes the sums very different. To help us find out why, it's time to introduce a special guest star...

YES INDEED, YOU LUCKY PEOPLE... FRESH FROM THE SEVENTEENTH CENTURY, MURDEROUS MATHS PROUDLY PRESENTS, IN PERSON, THE GREATEST EXPONENT OF HIGH-LIVING LOW-LIFE THAT HISTORY HAS EVER KNOWN...

THE CHEVALIER DE MERE!

I BET HE'S GOT GREEN PANTS ON

CHEERS

WILD APPLAUSE

It's impossible to have a book about chance without mentioning The Chevalier de Mere who spent his life betting on cards, dice, tossing coins and just about anything else you can think of. Chevy made a good living from all this until the year 1654 when he started a new little betting game that nearly broke him. The bet looked like a certain winner but in the end Chevy lost so much that he wrote to Blaise Pascal to ask why it kept going wrong. Pascal got very hooked on the subject of chance and soon lots of other top mathematicians of the day got involved too. Mind you, Pascal was the star because of his triangle.

Before The Chevalier started his losing game, he had made a lot of money with a simple rolling-die game. It worked something like this:

As we are on-the-case, brainy Murderous Maths types, it's not hard to see that Chevy was on to a good thing. (The people he was playing against must have had no maths sense at all!) However the chances of winning don't quite work out as you might imagine...

What is the chance of getting a six with one throw? It's $\frac{1}{6}$ of course.

What is the chance of getting at least one six with four throws? You might be tempted to think that it's $\frac{1}{6}+\frac{1}{6}+\frac{1}{6}+\frac{1}{6}$ which makes $\frac{4}{6}$ or $\frac{2}{3}$. In other words, for every three times The Chevalier played he should win two of them.

No, he wouldn't either because this way of adding up the chances of winning at dice are all wrong.

It becomes obvious why if you imagine the chance of getting a 6 in SIX throws. If you just added the chances you get $\frac{1}{6}+\frac{1}{6}+\frac{1}{6}+\frac{1}{6}+\frac{1}{6}+\frac{1}{6}$ which comes to 1. This would mean that if you throw a die six times you are absolutely 100% certain to get one six. Of course this isn't true. *If you throw a die six times you might not get any sixes or you might get more than one.* This is because the die has no memory! Every throw is independent of what has already happened.

Compare this with using our six playing cards. If the ace, 2, 3, 4, 5 and 6 are shuffled up and you pick them out one at a time (without replacing them) you must eventually get a six. *After picking all six cards, you MUST get a six ONE time only, no more and no less.* Picking the cards this way gives mutually exclusive results which is good news because…

If results are mutually exclusive then you can add the chances.

If The Chevalier played his game with six cards and picked out four of them, his chances of winning would indeed be $\frac{1}{6}+\frac{1}{6}+\frac{1}{6}+\frac{1}{6}$ which comes to $\frac{2}{3}$.

So tell me, Pascal, what are my chances of winning with the die?

We have to allow for the fact that you could throw forever and never get a six at all

So what we do is work out the chances of you not winning

How depressing!

This very clever idea makes this tricky sum much easier, so let's see how it works.

Two throws

Before we think about throwing the die four times, let's see the chances of The Chevalier getting a six in two throws. This is where the tree diagram starts to be really useful:

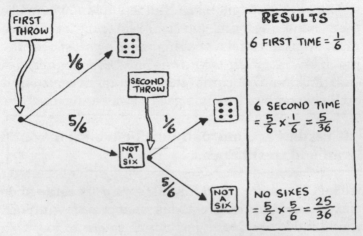

When The Chevalier first throws the die, the chance of a six is $\frac{1}{6}$, and the chance of *not* getting a six is $\frac{5}{6}$. If he doesn't get a six, then he throws again and the chances are the same. We can now use the tree diagram to see the chances of:

- Six on the first throw $= \frac{1}{6}$
- No six on the first throw but six on the second throw $= \frac{5}{6} \times \frac{1}{6} = \frac{5 \times 1}{6 \times 6} = \frac{5}{36}$
- No sixes on either throw $= \frac{5}{6} \times \frac{5}{6} = \frac{5 \times 5}{6 \times 6} = \frac{25}{36}$

These are the only three possible outcomes to the game. When you have all the possible outcomes to anything, they are mutually exclusive AND they must all add up to 1. If you know how fractions work you will find that $\frac{1}{6} + \frac{5}{36} + \frac{25}{36} = 1$ so that means the tree diagram works.

So what are The Chevalier's chances of getting a six on the first OR second throw? We could add these two chances together and get this rather ugly little sum: $\frac{1}{6}+\frac{5}{36}=\frac{11}{36}$. It's the right answer, but not much fun to work out.

The much easier way to get this answer is to see the chances of NOT getting a six on either throw. The diagram tells us this is $\frac{5}{6}\times\frac{5}{6}=\frac{25}{36}$. As the chances of NOT winning and the chances of winning must add up to 1, we can then say that the chances of winning are $1-\frac{25}{36}$. We can write 1 as $\frac{36}{36}$ so the sum now becomes $\frac{36}{36}-\frac{25}{36}=\frac{36-25}{36}=\frac{11}{36}$.

That's the answer we got before so it works. And it's a LOT simpler!

You can check these answers with a bit of common sense. The more times The Chevalier is allowed to throw the die, the more likely he is to get a six. We'll use percentages to see if our answers agree with this. If he just threw the die once, his chance of winning would be $\frac{1}{6}$ which is 16·67%. If he threw twice, his chance is $\frac{11}{36}$ which is 30·56% so yes, his chances have got better.

(Don't forget that The Chevalier wanted to win more times than he lost, so his chances had to be better than 50%. Just having two throws would never have given him a good enough chance of winning.)

III

There is another way of getting this result. Let's suppose that instead of throwing one die twice, the Chevalier threw two dice. (It gives the same answers.) We'll ask our artist Mr Reeve to draw out all the different outcomes that Chevy could get:

You'll see there are 36 possible outcomes all together. 25 of them don't have any sixes so they are losers, but there are 11 winners with at least one six. This shows the chance of winning to be $\frac{11}{36}$ which is what we worked out.

AHA! DRAWING OUT ALL THE COMBINATIONS IS MUCH EASIER THAN DOING THE SUMS!

OH REALLY? JUST WAIT TILL YOU SEE WHAT HAPPENS WITH THREE DICE!

The scalp collectors

REMEMBER URGUM AND GRIZELDA THROWING THE DIE THREE TIMES IN THE CAVE? NOW WE CAN WORK OUT WHO PROBABLY WON THE OTHER'S SCALP!

To get Urgum's scalp, Grizelda needed to throw a "one" with the die and she could try three times. Here's the tree diagram:

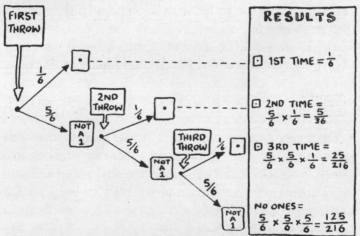

Now you *could* add together the chances of getting a "one" the first time, the second time and the third time and work out $\frac{1}{6} + \frac{5}{36} + \frac{25}{216}$, but why do such murderous sums when there's a much easier way?

The diagram shows the chance of NOT getting any ones in three throws is $\frac{5}{6} \times \frac{5}{6} \times \frac{5}{6} = \frac{125}{216}$. Therefore the chance of getting a one in three throws is $1 - \frac{125}{216} = \frac{216}{216} - \frac{125}{216} = \frac{91}{216}$.

Sums are much the easiest way to get the answer, and just to show what a bore it is to draw all the combinations out, we'll ask Mr Reeve do to it.

SHOVE OFF, POSKITT, YOU SILLY LITTLE MAN

Oooh deary dear … he's obviously feeling a bit grand today. He just wants to do posh pictures of dead famous people. Honestly, what are artists like? Give 'em a pencil and a desk to sit at and suddenly they think they're Reubens. At least printers are a decent bunch who don't throw little arty tantrums so we'll get them to print out all the 216 different combinations for us…

1,1,1 2,1,1 3,1,1 4,1,1 5,1,1 6,1,1 1,2,1 2,2,1 3,2,1 4,2,1 5,2,1 6,2,1 1,3,1

2,3,1 3,3,1 4,3,1 5,3,1 6,3,1 1,4,1 2,4,1 3,4,1 4,4,1 5,4,1 6,4,1 1,5,1 2,5,1

3,5,1 4,5,1 5,5,1 6,5,1 1,6,1 2,6,1 3,6,1 4,6,1 5,6,1 6,6,1 1,1,2 2,1,2 3,1,2

4,1,2 5,1,2 6,1,2 1,2,2 2,2,2 3,2,2 4,2,2 5,2,2 6,2,2 1,3,2 2,3,2 3,3,2 4,3,2

5,3,2 6,3,2 1,4,2 2,4,2 3,4,2 4,4,2 5,4,2 6,4,2 1,5,2 2,5,2 3,5,2 4,5,2 5,5,2

6,5,2 1,6,2 2,6,2 3,6,2 4,6,2 5,6,2 6,6,2 1,1,3 2,1,3 3,1,3 4,1,3 5,1,3 6,1,3

1,2,3 2,2,3 3,2,3 4,2,3 5,2,3 6,2,3 1,3,3 2,3,3 3,3,3 4,3,3 5,3,3 6,3,3 1,4,3

2,4,3 3,4,3 4,4,3 5,4,3 6,4,3 1,5,3 2,5,3 3,5,3 4,5,3 5,5,3 6,5,3 1,6,3 2,6,3

3,6,3 4,6,3 5,6,3 6,6,3 1,1,4 2,1,4 3,1,4 4,1,4 5,1,4 6,1,4 1,2,4 2,2,4 3,2,4

4,2,4 5,2,4 6,2,4 1,3,4 2,3,4 3,3,4 4,3,4 5,3,4 6,3,4 1,4,4 2,4,4 3,4,4 4,4,4

5,4,4 6,4,4 1,5,4 2,5,4 3,5,4 4,5,4 5,5,4 6,5,4 1,6,4 2,6,4 3,6,4 4,6,4 5,6,4

6,6,4 1,1,5 2,1,5 3,1,5 4,1,5 5,1,5 6,1,5 1,2,5 2,2,5 3,2,5 4,2,5 5,2,5 6,2,5

1,3,5 2,3,5 3,3,5 4,3,5 5,3,5 6,3,5 1,4,5 2,4,5 3,4,5 4,4,5 5,4,5 6,4,5 1,5,5

2,5,5 3,5,5 4,5,5 5,5,5 6,5,5 1,6,5 2,6,5 3,6,5 4,6,5 5,6,5 6,6,5 1,1,6 2,1,6

3,1,6 4,1,6 5,1,6 6,1,6 1,2,6 2,2,6 3,2,6 4,2,6 5,2,6 6,2,6 1,3,6 2,3,6 3,3,6

4,3,6 5,3,6 6,3,6 1,4,6 2,4,6 3,4,6 4,4,6 5,4,6 6,4,6 1,5,6 2,5,6 3,5,6 4,5,6

5,5,6 6,5,6 1,6,6 2,6,6 3,6,6 4,6,6 5,6,6 6,6,6

You've now got to go through and count up all the combinations with a "1" in them to get Grizelda's chances of winning. (Go on, get counting, you know you want to.) You should find that the sums are correct and that there are 91 of them. But be honest, the maths is quicker!

When you finish up with answers like $\frac{91}{216}$ and $\frac{125}{216}$ they look clearer if you convert them into percentages. Here's how they turn out:

- Grizelda only had a 42·13% chance of getting Urgum's scalp.

- Urgum had a 57·87% chance of getting Grizelda's scalp which was much better!

The Chevalier's four throws

Now we've decided that the maths works, we can see that Chevy's chance of NOT getting any sixes in four throws was $\frac{5}{6} \times \frac{5}{6} \times \frac{5}{6} \times \frac{5}{6}$ which comes to $\frac{625}{1296}$ and works out to be 48·23%. So his chance of winning his bet by getting at least one six in four throws was $100\% - 48·23\% = 51·77\%$. Although this means that Chevy was winning only slightly more often than he was losing, it was enough for him to make a lot of money over the years!

The Chevalier's losing double dice game

Although the Chevalier was winning only about 52 times out of every 100 times that he played his "four throws" game, he played so much that people got fed up with him slowly but surely taking their money. He decided to invent a new game.

Let's see why Chevy thought he could win at this game. First of all, we have to know the chances of throwing a double six with ONE throw.

- The first die can land in six different ways, and the second die can also land in six different ways. This means that the total number of different ways the two dice can land is 6×6 which comes to 36.

- Only one of these ways has both dice showing "six" so the chance of throwing a double six in one throw is $\frac{1}{36}$.

If you want to check this, look back to page 112 where all the 36 combinations for two dice are written out. You'll see that only one gives double six.

So if Chevy's chance of a double six in one throw is $\frac{1}{36}$, what are his chances in 24 throws?

No! What Chevy thought was that if he threw 24 times the chances would be $\frac{1}{36} + \frac{1}{36} + \frac{1}{36} + \dots$ twenty four times, but as we found out with his first die game, this is wrong.

What you have to do is work out the chances of *not* getting a double six. On the first throw this is $\frac{35}{36}$, and so for 24 throws this is $\frac{35}{36} \times \frac{35}{36} \times \frac{35}{36} \times$ ... twenty-four times. This is a LOT easier to write as $(\frac{35}{36})^{24}$ or you can put $\frac{35^{24}}{36^{24}}$ if you prefer. By now you'll have already worked this sum out in your head and converted it to a percentage to find: the chances of *not* getting a double six in 24 throws is 50·86%.

In other words, out of 100 goes at this game, the chances are that he would lose about 51 times and only win 49 times. If he kept playing this same game on and on and on (and he did!) ... bye bye trousers.

By the way, if he had allowed himself one extra go at throwing a double six – making 25 goes altogether – he should have very slowly started to win. (Roughly speaking it works out that in 99 games he could expect to lose 49 times and win 50.)

Using dice in other games

Quite a lot of games depend on throwing two dice, so it's interesting to look at all the combinations back on page 112 again.

There are two obvious things to see to start with:

- There is only one way of throwing each "double" such as 2-2.
- There are two ways of throwing all the other combinations such as 5-3 and 3-5.

Usually when you throw two dice you add up the spots to see what total number you get. The smallest total you can get is 2, which comes from throwing 1-1. The largest total is 12 from throwing 6-6.

What is important is that some totals are far more likely to occur than others! If you count up the spots on each pair of dice, you'll find the ways of throwing each total are as follows:

Total	Ways	Combinations
2	1	1-1
3	2	1-2, 2-1
4	3	1-3, 2-2, 3-1
5	4	1-4, 2-3, 3-2, 4-1
6	5	1-5, 2-4, 3-3, 4-2, 5-1
7	6	1-6, 2-5, 3-4, 4-3, 5-2, 6-1
8	5	2-6, 3-5, 4-4, 5-3, 6-2
9	4	3-6, 4-5, 5-4, 6-3
10	3	4-6, 5-5, 6-4
11	2	5-6, 6-5
12	1	6-6

From this you can see that throwing a total of 7 is the most likely result because there are 6 ways it can be made with the two dice. 2 and 12 are the most unlikely because there is only one way of making each of them. This sort of information would have come in very handy for Chevy.

It's not hard to see why Chevy would win. Out of the 36 possible combinations, 4 combinations add up to five, 5 add up to six, 6 add up to 7 and 5 add up to 8. This means that there are $4+5+6+5=20$ winning combinations for Chevy. As there are 36 combinations altogether, his chances would be $\frac{20}{36}$ which are 55·56%. He's on to a winner!

Go directly to jail

One of the favourite subjects for people studying chance is the board game "Monopoly". If you don't know it, what happens is that you all start with £1,500 of pretend money and you go round the board buying up squares and then charging each other rent for landing on them. It all begins in a nice friendly fashion, and then three hours later people are shouting and weeping, hurling bits all round the room, snatching each other's cards, stealing money from the bank and in the corner the cat is quietly choking on a miniature top hat. It's marvellous fun.

All sorts of people have spent long hours on computers deciding which is "the second-most-landed-on square in Monopoly". In keeping with the spirit of the game this leads to some interesting academic discussions...

One thing they do agree on is the most-landed-on square which is "Jail/Just Visiting". There are several ways of ending IN jail, but one of them is of special interest to us right now. When you play Monopoly you throw two dice and if you get a double you throw again. However, if you throw THREE doubles in a row, you're nicked. So what are the chances of throwing three doubles?

As there are 36 ways the dice can fall and 6 of them are doubles, then the chances of throwing the dice once and getting a double are $\frac{6}{36}$ which is $\frac{1}{6}$. A quick tree diagram shows what happens with three throws:

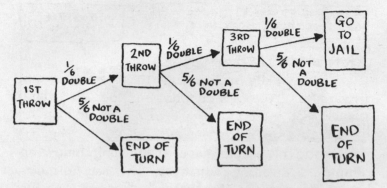

If you work along the diagram towards the "Go to Jail" outcome the chances are $\frac{1}{6} \times \frac{1}{6} \times \frac{1}{6} = \frac{1}{216}$. This tells us that every 216 turns you take in Monopoly, on one of them you can expect to throw three doubles and land in jail.

Once you're in jail you have three chances to throw a double to get out, otherwise you need to pay a £50 fine (or use a "Get out of Jail" card). If you're allowed three tries, what are the chances of throwing a double?

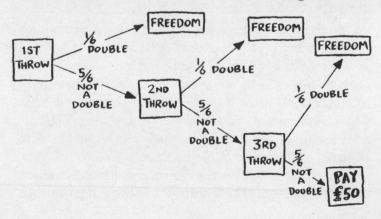

On the diagram, you can see it's more obvious to work out the chances of having to pay the fine, which are $\frac{5}{6} \times \frac{5}{6} \times \frac{5}{6}$ making $\frac{125}{216}$. So your chances of getting a double in three tries are $\frac{91}{216}$.

Brett and Lil's Vicious Circle!

Here's a deadly game that Brett Shuffler and Riverboat Lil play after sundown in the Last Chance Saloon. You can make your own version and the fun part is that the more you know about dice then the better you'll be! First you need to make a playboard like this (but bigger of course):

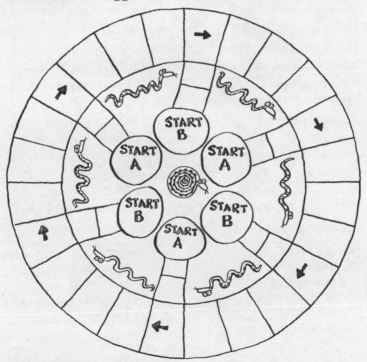

You also need three counters each and two dice.

- The counters are put on the start squares. The two players take turns to throw the two dice.
- After throwing the dice, a player chooses which counter he wants to move. (If he only has one left, then he has to move it!) The counter must be moved the exact total shown on the two dice and they all go in the same direction. Once a counter has been moved on to the main circle, it goes round until it is killed off or the game ends.

I'M NOT ALLOWED TO LAND ON ONE OF MY OWN COUNTERS...

BUT IF I LAND ON ONE OF BRETT'S COUNTERS, THAT COUNTER IS KILLED OFF THE BOARD

KEEP GOING ROUND AND ROUND...

AND THE LAST COUNTER LEFT ON THE BOARD WINS

There is a lot of skill in this game which you'll work out as you go along. Here's a clue to start you off:

TRY TO MAKE SURE YOU **NEVER** LEAVE A COUNTER SEVEN SQUARES IN FRONT OF THE ENEMY

BECAUSE SEVEN IS THE MOST LIKELY NUMBER AND YOU'LL BE KILLED OFF

When you are familiar with what to expect from throwing dice, you'll find that you have an advantage in all sorts of games such as Ludo, Monopoly, Sorry and especially backgammon!

Unbelievable birthdays

You are suddenly stranded on a desert island with no hope of rescue for a whole year. What beastly luck! All there is to entertain you are long beaches, deep blue sea, free discos and go-karting, unlimited video games, burger trees, curry bushes and 30 of your absolute very best friends.

The only way to take your mind off the grim situation is to have as many parties as possible. All your 30 friends announce that they will each have a party on their birthday. This sounds great but there's one nasty thought – what if two of them have the same birthday? But as there are 365 days in a year, it's not very likely any parties will clash. Or is it?

This is *spooky*! Here are how the sums look and it's one of those things where it's easier to work out the chances of everybody's birthday *not* being the same to start with. Let's imagine your friends all lined up:

- Your first friend can have a birthday on any of the 365 days in the year. We can call this a chance of $\frac{365}{365}$ which works out as a chance of 1. What we're saying here is that it is absolutely 100% certain that the first friend hasn't got the same birthday as anyone else, because so far there isn't anybody else!

- What are the chances of your second friend having *the same* birthday as the first? It's $\frac{1}{365}$, so the chances of a different birthday are $\frac{364}{365}$.

- Providing the first two people have different birthdays, what are the chances of your third friend having the same birthday as one of them? It's $\frac{2}{365}$, so the chances that your third friend has a different birthday are $\frac{363}{365}$.

In the same way as we dealt with the dice, we can find the chances of your first three friends all having different birthdays. Here's the tree diagram:

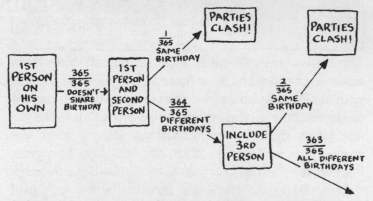

As you can see, we just multiply the chances of *not* having the same birthday together, so it's $\frac{365}{365} \times \frac{364}{365} \times \frac{363}{365}$. This comes to 99·18% which means it is extremely likely all three birthdays will be different. Let's bring in your fourth friend.

- After the first three friends, there are only 362 days on which the fourth person can have another different birthday, so the chance is $\frac{362}{365}$.

- Person number five's chances of having a different birthday altogether are $\frac{361}{365}$.

You can see the pattern now. You get a sum that starts like this: $\frac{365}{365} \times \frac{364}{365} \times \frac{363}{365} \times \frac{362}{365} \times \ldots$ and ends like this $\ldots \times \frac{338}{365} \times \frac{337}{365} \times \frac{336}{365}$

If you want to be slick, you can write it as $\frac{365!}{(365)^{30} \times 335!}$

By now you might be drooling with excitement as you recall how nicely the combination sums all cancelled themselves out. Sorry to disappoint you, but this doesn't work out quite so nicely. You need to have a good old bash on the calculator but in the end you should find the sum comes to 0·29368 which converts to 29·37%. So the chance of 30 people all having different birthdays is slightly less than 30% which means: if you have 30 friends, there is more than a 70% chance that at least two of them share a birthday!

Sadly this means that on your desert island it's unlikely that you will be able to get to everybody's birthday party – unless you're a mad-for-it crazy dude and go to more than one party in a day. Wahey!

If you get a big bit of paper and a calculator you can work out what happens with smaller or larger groups of people. The chances of two people sharing a birthday in a group run like this:

Number of people in group	Chance of at least two people sharing a birthday (roughly)
5	2·71%
10	11·7%
15	25%
20	41%
23	51%
25	57%
30	71%
35	81%

Having a group of 23 people is interesting because that's the smallest group you can have where it's more likely than not that two people will share a birthday. By the way, if you have 100 people the chances that every single person has a different birthday are about 1 in *3 million*.

The devious decks

A normal deck of playing cards has 52 cards divided equally into four "suits" called spades, hearts, clubs and diamonds, giving 13 cards in each suit. (There might also be one or two "jokers" in the pack but they hardly ever get used.) Playing cards are so popular that at any time of day or night, all over the world, millions of people are playing games with them. A lot of these games such as whist and bridge involve four people sitting round a table, and they shuffle up the deck then deal all the cards out so they get 13 cards each. The interesting bit for us is that once or twice a year there is a newspaper report saying this has happened:

So how likely is it that one person gets all 13 spades? There are lots of ways of approaching this sum, but the most straightforward is to imagine that you are being passed your cards one at a time. (The chances are exactly the same as if you are being dealt your 13 cards in the normal way.)

- There are 13 spades in the deck of 52 cards, so the chances of your first card being a spade are $\frac{13}{52}$.
- There are 51 cards left in the deck, but only 12 of them are spades because you've already got one. So the chances that the second card will be a spade are $\frac{12}{51}$.

- By now there are only 50 cards left in the deck and only 11 of them are spades, so for your third card the chances of a spade are $\frac{11}{50}$. (So far, the chances of your first three cards being spades are: $\frac{13}{52} \times \frac{12}{51} \times \frac{11}{50}$ which comes to about 1·29% so it's already pretty unlikely.)
- The chances of your fourth card being a spade are $\frac{10}{49}$, and your fifth card's chances are $\frac{9}{48}$ and so on...
- Finally the chances of your 13th card being the last spade are $\frac{1}{40}$. (Even if your first 12 cards have all been spades, it's a bit sad to think that there's only a 1 in 40 chance of your thirteenth card being the last one!)

So here's the chances of all your cards being spades:

$$\frac{13 \times 12 \times 11 \times 10 \times 9 \times 8 \times 7 \times 6 \times 5 \times 4 \times 3 \times 2 \times 1}{52 \times 51 \times 50 \times 49 \times 48 \times 47 \times 46 \times 45 \times 44 \times 43 \times 42 \times 41 \times 40}$$

This is a lot easier to write out as $\frac{13! \times 39!}{52!}$ and it comes to $\frac{1}{635,013,559,600}$.

THE CHANCES ARE ABOUT ONE IN 635 BILLION!

GREAT THUNDERING PANTS!

SNIGGERING TITTER

So the odds of getting all 13 spades are quite incredible, but be warned – the chances of this happening are far more likely:

Yes, it's a fact that if you're playing cards with *that* sort of person and you have to nip into the kitchen to get some cheese straws, the chances of getting 13 spades are about 98% because they'll fiddle the cards while you're away. Either that, or when you sit down you'll land on a whoopee cushion.

If you prefer combinations...
Another way to work out the chances of getting 13 spades is to think about combinations. There are 52 cards in the pack, how many combinations of 13 cards are there? If you look back to page 93, you'll see we can write the number of combinations as $^{52}C_{13}$ which is $\frac{52!}{13! \times 39!}$. Surprise surprise, this comes to 635,013,559,600. As only one of these combinations gives us all the 13 spades, the chances are 1 in 635,013,559,600 which is what we had before.

Other card chances
All 13 cards the same suit
If you're not fussy which suit all your 13 cards are, then as well as spades you'd be happy with all hearts, all diamonds or all clubs. This means that out of all the combinations there are FOUR which would make you happy so your chances of all 13

cards being the same are 4 in 635,013,559,600. This comes to 1 in 158,753,389,900.

All 13 spades in the correct order
What are the chances of the first card you get being the ace of spades? It's $\frac{1}{52}$. Then the  chances of the next card being the 2 of spades is $\frac{1}{51}$ and the chances of the 3 being next are $\frac{1}{50}$ and so on until the chances of the king coming 13th are $\frac{1}{40}$. The sum turns out to be $\frac{1}{52 \times 51 \times 50 \times 49 \times 48 \times 47 \times 46 \times 45 \times 44 \times 43 \times 42 \times 41 \times 40}$ which you can write as $\frac{39!}{52!}$ If you battle it through with your calculator you'll find the chances are roughly 1 in 3,954,242,643,910,000,000,000.

All four players getting one complete suit each
If you were getting bored of these silly little sums with small numbers, welcome to the big time! Imagine the deck is shuffled, then the first player is given thirteen cards one at a time.

- What are the chances that the first player gets a complete suit? As we know, it's 1 in 158,753,389,900.
- Now we work out the second player's chances of a complete suit. The first card can be any of the 39 cards left. The second card must be the same suit and there are 12 suitable cards out of the remaining 38 cards left giving a chance of $\frac{12}{38}$. Then there are 11 cards from the remaining 37 and so on. The chances of the second player getting a complete suit are:

$$\frac{12 \times 11 \times 10 \times 9 \times 8 \times 7 \times 6 \times 5 \times 4 \times 3 \times 2 \times 1}{38 \times 37 \times 36 \times 35 \times 34 \times 33 \times 32 \times 31 \times 30 \times 29 \times 28 \times 27}$$

Which is $\frac{12! \times 26!}{38!}$ and comes to 1 in 2,707,475,148.

- The third player starts getting cards. The first can be any of the 26 cards left, then the second can be any of the 12 of the same suit left in the pack of 25. Then it's $\frac{11}{24}$ then $\frac{10}{23}$ ... and on we go again to get the chances of the third player getting a complete suit:

$$\frac{12 \times 11 \times 10 \times 9 \times 8 \times 7 \times 6 \times 5 \times 4 \times 3 \times 2 \times 1}{25 \times 24 \times 23 \times 22 \times 21 \times 20 \times 19 \times 18 \times 17 \times 16 \times 15 \times 14}$$

Which is $\frac{12! \times 13!}{25!}$ and comes to 1 in 5,200,300.

- Finally the fourth player starts getting cards. There are only 13 cards left, and of course the other three suits have already gone. So what are the chances of getting all 13 cards the same suit? It's 1. Phew, thank goodness for that!

To get the chances of all four people each getting a complete suit we multiply the four chances together and get $\frac{1}{158,753,389,900} \times \frac{1}{2,707,475,148} \times \frac{1}{5,200,300} \times \frac{1}{1}$ which comes to about 1 chance in 2,235,197,406,900, 000,000,000,000,000.

And now brace yourself for the biggest sum in this book:

For every player to get one suit each in the correct order, every card in the pack has to be in the right order. In other words, out of all the permutations that the pack of cards can have, only ONE of them will do. So how many permutations are we talking about? Easy, it's 52! so the chance of everybody getting what they want is 1 in 52!. It works out to be roughly 1 in 80,000,000,000,000,000,000,000,000,

000,000,000,000,000,000,000,000,000,000,000,000, 000,000. (There are 67 zeros there.)

Don't even try to imagine how big this number is or your brain will melt. But just to give you a vague idea:

- Suppose everybody in the whole world sat down in groups of four.
- And each group dealt out a pack of cards *every second*.

The chances are that all four people in one of the groups would each get the suit they wanted in the correct order once in about two thousand million million million million million million million million years. In numbers this looks like: 2,000,000,000,000,000, 000,000,000,000,000,000,000,000,000,000,000. And just to give you an idea how long this is, the earth is only 4,500,000,000 years old and dinosaurs died out 65,000,000 years ago.

How to make your own little bit of history
1 Get a pack of cards.
2 Shuffle it well.
3 Look through the pack and see the order they have finished in.
4 Think to yourself...

I BET THAT IN THE WHOLE HISTORY OF THE UNIVERSE NOBODY EVER HAS OR EVER WILL SHUFFLE CARDS INTO THAT ORDER AGAIN!

Satisfying, isn't it?

The "Yarborough" insurance

Lord Yarborough used to be a famous card player and he knew how irritating it was to pick up a hand of 13 cards and find there was not one high value card among them. So he set up a sort of insurance scheme for card players whereby you paid him £1, but if your hand had nothing higher than a nine, he would pay you £1,000 back. His friends quite often took him up on this offer, probably just for the fun of it as much as anything else – but did Lord Yarborough win or lose?

We can work it out. You would miss out on the £1,000 prize if you had an ace, King, Queen, Jack or 10 in your hand. As there are four of each of these cards in the pack, that means there are 20 cards you don't want. So when you get your first card, your chance is $\frac{32}{52}$ that it's a card valued at nine or less. For your second card the chance is $\frac{31}{51}$, for the third card it's $\frac{30}{50}$ and so on until the chance for your 13th card is $\frac{20}{40}$. The whole sum ends up as $\frac{32! \times 39!}{19! \times 52!}$ which comes down to $\frac{1}{1828}$. In other words for every £1,000 he paid out, Lord Yarborough should have collected £1,828. Nice one!

(Mind you, don't forget that in all these sums we are only working out what *should* happen. If Lord Yarborough was having bad luck, he could have lost more than he won!)

DO YOU PAY OUT IF I'VE GOT 'MR BUN THE BAKER'?

When meteors collide and monkeys type

Some things in life are so unlikely that you'd think they were impossible. Think about these:

- At breakfast you knock over the cereal packet, and when the crispies fall all over the floor they just happen to spell out your name.

- Everybody in the whole country suddenly fancies a day out at your local park, and the traffic jams go back for 100 miles in every direction. The streets are full of people standing on each others heads to make room and what's more, all the pipes under the streets have burst because everybody in the town used the toilets all at once!

- Or even ... a giant meteor is hurtling towards Earth and it is destined to land slap bang on your front doorstep. The whole of life as we know it will be ended!

Unlikely – yes. But impossible? NO! However, even if a meteor was heading towards your doorstep, don't panic. A second meteor could come screaming in from the opposite direction at the exact speed and at the exact time and knock the first one out of the way. Either that, or everyone in China might just happen to look up and sneeze at the same time and blast Earth out of the way. It's not impossible.

When the unlikely should happen

What are your chances of being struck by lightning? People love thinking about this sum and generally they agree it's about 1 chance in 600,000. This means that you personally are extremely unlikely to be zapped. However if you have a list of 600,000 people, the chances are that one of them WILL be zapped and that one person might feel it is very unfair. Sadly, that's how the laws of chance work and there's no way of getting out of it.

I WANTED TO BE A BUS CONDUCTOR, NOT A LIGHTNING CONDUCTOR!

Some years ago a man complained to the national lottery because he had bought over 800 tickets and never had even a tiny win. The lottery had claimed (correctly) that 1 ticket in every 54 should win something, but the man insisted that they had been lying and demanded all his money back. So what were his chances of *not* winning at all? (It's the same sort of sum as when The Chevalier was throwing his dice a few times and we asked what were his chances of NOT getting a six?)

His chances of the first ticket NOT winning were $\frac{53}{54}$, the chances of the second ticket NOT winning were $\frac{53}{54}$ and so on for 800 tickets. Just like Chevy's dice, we multiply $\frac{53}{54} \times \frac{53}{54} \times \frac{53}{54} \times$ ... 800 times which we can write as $(\frac{53}{54})^{800}$. The answer tells us that the chance of none of the 800 tickets winning is roughly 1 in 3,000,000. This is a tiny chance, but when you think about all the millions of people that buy lottery tickets, there *was* a slim chance that someone would be incredibly unsuccessful and it was him. The man had been very unlucky but he should have realized that's what lotteries are all about – luck!

Monkeys and typewriters

There is an old probability theory that says: Give 100,000 monkeys a typewriter each and shut them in a room. Let them tap away at the keys, and if you come back after a million years, by chance one of them will have written the whole of Shakespeare's play *Hamlet*.

Although this theory at first seems cute and lovely, it turns out to be quite horrific. As any Murderous

Maths reader will realize, if you leave 100,000 monkeys shut in a room and you come back after a million years – *think of the smell*! After the monkeys discover that they can't eat typewriters, they will end up well-dead, rotted and infested with maggots.

Even if your monkeys did survive and kept tapping away, who is going to check all the trillions of bits of paper? And can you imagine the frustration of it?

So instead of getting 100,000 real monkeys, let's test this theory with a bit of maths. First we'll fix up a typewriter so that it only has the 26 letter and 10

number keys, then we'll bring in one monkey called Oswald. Let's say Oswald bangs one letter or number key every second. After ten seconds we might get:

d j v n s d 8 3 2 h

or...

P P 4 l m 1 x x x s

What are the chances that Oswald might start writing this book? We won't be fussy about capital letters or punctuation or spaces so starting with the title his first fourteen letters would have to be this:

do you feel lucky

As there are 36 letter and number keys on the typewriter, the chances of him getting the first "d" are $\frac{1}{36}$. The chances of him then hitting "o" are $\frac{1}{36}$ and so on. So the chances of Oswald typing "doyoufeellucky" in the first fourteen seconds are $\frac{1}{36} \times \frac{1}{36} \times \frac{1}{36} \times \ldots$ and so on fourteen times which is $\frac{1}{36^{14}}$. This works out roughly as 1 chance in 6,000,000,000,000,000,000,000,000.

Let's suppose we let Oswald have more than one attempt. We know that the chances are he'll only get "doyoufeellucky" once in 36^{14} attempts, so if each attempt takes 14 seconds, how long will this take? In seconds it's 14×36^{14} which comes to about 84,000,000,000,000,000,000,000,000 seconds. Let's convert this to years by dividing by the number of seconds in a year.

The number of seconds in a year is 60 seconds in a minute $\times$ 60 minutes in an hour $\times$ 24 hours in a day $\times$ 365 days in a year, so you get $60 \times 60 \times 24 \times 365 = 31,536,000$. We'll call this 30,000,000 to keep things simple.

It turns out that Oswald will need to keep typing for 2,800,000,000,000,000 years.

Poor Oswald, the least we can do is get some more monkeys to help him. The trouble is that even if we get 100,000 monkeys, the chances are that only ONE of them would type "doyoufeellucky" ONCE in **twenty-eight thousand million years**.

So how many monkeys and how many millions of years do you think it would take to write this whole book?

HUH! I RECKON IT TOOK ONE HALF-WITTED MONKEY ABOUT TEN MINUTES...

Making pie with a cocktail stick

Here's a murderous calculation – but we can make it much simpler *with a bit of luck*!

- Get something that is perfectly round such as a mug or a coin.
- Measure round the outside. (It's best to do this by putting some string right round it, then holding the string against a ruler.) This is called the "circumference".
- Measure the diameter – which is the distance across the centre.
- Divide the circumference by the diameter.
- It doesn't matter what size of circle you start with (it could be a round dustbin or just a tiny coin), your answer should be just over 3.
- If you do this really accurately, you'll find your answer is about $3\frac{1}{7}$.
- If you do this unbelievably accurately, your answer might be 3·1416.
- If you do this impossibly accurately, your answer should be about 3·14159265...

The more accurately you do this measurement, then the more decimal places you'll be able to work out, but of course there are limits to how accurate you can be. If you really wanted to, you could measure right round the whole earth and then drill a hole through the middle and measure the diameter. If you made your measurements accurate to the nearest thousandth of a millimetre – you might get an

143

answer of 3·141592653589793 … but it still wouldn't be *exactly* right!

The exact answer is impossible to write down, so instead it has a special sign "π". This is the ancient Greek letter called "pi" (which sounds like "pie") and for thousands of years mathematicians have been battling away to work out the exact value of π. They have come up with some amazing ways of calculating it and here are some of the formulas they used:

$$\pi = 3 \times \left(1 + \frac{(1^2)}{4 \times 6} + \frac{(1^2 \times 3^2)}{4 \times 6 \times 8 \times 10} + \frac{(1^2 \times 3^2 \times 5^2)}{4 \times 6 \times 8 \times 10 \times 12 \times 14} + \cdots \right)$$

$$\frac{\pi}{2} = \frac{2 \times 2 \times 4 \times 4 \times 6 \times 6 \times 8 \times 8 \times 10 \times \ldots}{1 \times 3 \times 3 \times 5 \times 5 \times 7 \times 7 \times 9 \times \ 9 \ \times \ldots}$$

or even: $\frac{\pi}{4} = \arctan\left(\frac{1}{2}\right) + \arctan\left(\frac{1}{3}\right)$

…which is all very handy as long as you know what an "arctan" is. It sounds like the sort of thing your uncle Sidney might have rusting away in his shed so just give it a squirt of oil and a rub down with a soft cloth and who knows, there might be a few calculations left in it after all.

AND YOU'RE QUITE SURE THIS IS AN ARCTAN?

What's luck got to do with it?

As strange as it may seem, there are times when the most murderous of problems can be solved by using the laws of chance. When pure mathematicians start wondering about colossal numbers with millions of digits, there are methods which even involve throwing dice to solve their sums! Using probability to solve sums can get a bit complicated but for working out π there's a nice simple method that we can all understand.

The classic way of doing this sum is to have a floor which has floorboards that you can see. The important thing is that the cracks between the floorboards are all very thin, and they are all exactly the same width apart. You also need a thin stick (such as a cocktail stick) which is exactly the same length as the width of a floorboard.

If you don't have floorboards (or if you can't see them because your floor is covered in magazines, old socks, pizza boxes, mould, soggy crisps, grass clippings and pants) then you can always get a large piece of paper and draw lines across it that are the same distance apart. They don't have to be as wide as floorboards – 5cm will do. You then get a cocktail stick or a match which is 5cm long or whatever the width you've used is and you're ready.

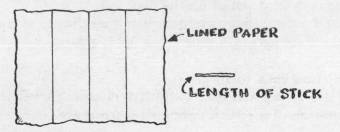

LINED PAPER

LENGTH OF STICK

Here's what you do:

- Hold your stick above the floor at a reasonable height and pointing downwards. Drop it. Pick it up and drop it again. And again. And again...
- Count how many times you drop the stick.
- Also count how many times the stick lands touching one of the cracks. (Even if the end of the stick is only just over a crack, that counts.)

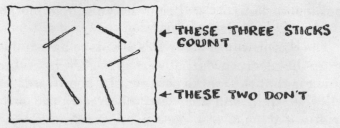

← THESE THREE STICKS COUNT

← THESE TWO DON'T

- When you've dropped your stick lots of times (say 100 times), do this sum:
- Multiply the number of times you dropped the stick by 2.
- Divide by the number of times the stick fell on a crack.
- This should give you a value for π!

Suppose you drop your stick 100 times and it lands on a crack 64 times. The sum you work out is 2 × 100 which is 200, then divide that by 64 to get 3·125. That's not a bad result for π when all you've done is drop a stick on the floor, is it?

Of course, the more times you drop the stick, then the more accurate your value for π will be.

So how does this work?

This calculation uses two ways of seeing what the chances of the stick falling on a crack are.

- The first way is the *experimental* way. We actually dropped the stick and counted up the results, and we found that out of 100 drops, it landed on a crack 64 times. So our experiment showed that the chances of it landing on a crack are $\frac{64}{100}$.

- The second way is the *mathematical* way which comes about like this: the chances of the stick landing on a crack rely on where the centre of the stick falls and what direction the stick is turned in. If you think about the stick turning round, you can see there's some sort of circle involved and although the sums are rather nasty, the maths eventually tells you that the chance of the stick falling on a crack is $\frac{2}{\pi}$.

As these two answers are both for the same thing (the chances of the stick landing on a crack), they should equal each other so we get the result:

$$\frac{2}{\pi} = \frac{64}{100}$$

If you know about equations then you'll know that you can turn both sides of the equation upside down and get $\frac{\pi}{2} = \frac{100}{64}$ and then you multiply both sides by 2 to get:

$$\pi = \frac{2 \times 100}{64} = \frac{200}{64} = 3{\cdot}125$$

Can you rely on this method?

No! That's what makes experiments in chance such fun. If you just drop the stick 10 times, you'll get a very rough value of π if you're lucky. If you drop the stick 100 times you're more likely to get a better value of π. If you drop the stick 1,000 times you're almost certain to get quite a good value of π – but there is no guarantee!

It might even be that you drop the stick *one million* times and it never lands on a crack! There's no reason why that couldn't happen. But if it does – make sure to look out of the window. On a day like that, those asteroids are bound to collide, which will be well worth watching.

Adding adders

Can you imagine coming across a pond full of
lethal snakes and having to find out how many
there are? You're going to have to count some of
them, but wouldn't it be nice if you didn't have to
count them all?

Believe it or not, you can get a close answer with a
couple of sums and bit of luck. The method is called
"sampling" and it works something like this...

150

YOU SEE, BRETT, WITH A BIT OF LUCK, WHEN WE THREW THE 20 PAINTED ONES BACK THEY'LL HAVE GOT ALL MIXED UP WITH THE OTHERS GOOD AND PROPER...

AND NOW WE'VE PULLED OUT 4 PAINTED AND 12 PLAIN

SO THE CHANCES ARE FOR EVERY ONE SNAKE YOU PAINTED THERE'S THREE YOU DIDN'T

AND WITH A BIT OF LUCK, THAT APPLIES TO EVERY SNAKE IN THE POND

SO IN THE WHOLE POND, IF THERE'S 20 PAINTED SNAKES THERE SHOULD BE ABOUT 20×3 SNAKES WITHOUT PAINT. THAT MAKES 60 PLAIN ONES

MAKING IT ABOUT 80 SNAKES ALTOGETHER...

Some odd odds

The sock drawer

Did you ever have a night when these two things happened at once...

- You are suddenly invited to a very posh party for which you HAVE TO WEAR clean, matching socks. (Oh, and trousers, shirt, shoes etc.)
- All your socks are so dirty that you can't tell what colour they are until you wash them.

You fumble under your bed and find 20 socks which all look the same, even though they are supposed to be 10 different-coloured pairs.

If you pick out two socks and wash them, what are the chances that you'll get a matching pair?

The strange answer is 1 in 19.

The first sock you pull out could be *any* of the 20 socks. Of the 19 socks left, only one will match the first one, so the chances of getting it are 1 in 19.

The spider tank

You are working in a pet shop and the spider tank has 20 spiders in it. Ten of them are Diamond Toed Oxdroppers, and ten are Yellow Hooded Widowmakers. Old Auntie Crystal Fogsworth comes in and asks for a matching pair to put in her husband's slippers for a laugh. Just as you reach into the tank – there's a power cut.

How many spiders do you have to pull out before you are sure of getting a matching pair?

If you're lucky, the first two will match.

If you're unlucky then the first two will be different so you'll have to pull out a third. This third spider must match one of the other two, so the answer is that at most you need to pull out three spiders.

Suppose Auntie Crystal decides that she wants two Widowmakers? How many spiders might you have to pull out now?

The first ten spiders you pull out might all be the Oxdroppers, so then you have to go on and grab two Widowmakers. Therefore the answer is that you might have to pull out twelve spiders – if you survive that long.

The geography test
Holy pants! You turn up at a geog lesson and are suddenly presented with a test paper of 15 questions.

Each question gives you 4 answers to choose from but there's just one problem: you usually spend geog lessons doing things like counting the hairs on your head or trying to take your socks off without using your hands.

> Question 1:
> What is the population of Nmbonga Island?
> A – 871, B – 872, C – 873, D – 874

Of course you haven't the foggiest idea, so you have to guess. Your chances of getting it right are 1 in 4 or $\frac{1}{4}$.

All the other questions are equally baffling, but what are the chances of guessing all 15 answers correctly?

It's $\frac{1}{4} \times \frac{1}{4} \times \frac{1}{4} \times \ldots$ fifteen times. This comes to $\frac{1}{4^{15}}$ which is $\frac{1}{1,073,741,824}$. In other words your chances of guessing your way to geographical geniusness are less than 1 in one thousand million.

Mind you, if you worked these chances out yourself, who cares about geog? Maths is a much cooler subject because without it nobody could have counted up the population of Nmbonga in the first place.

A die and a deck

You throw a die and pick a card from a full pack. What are the chances that the die lands on 3 OR 4 AND the card you pick is a heart?

We could start wuffling on here about independent and exclusive events, but when you've got two separate things happening there's a neat short cut

which just about explains itself. It's called a
probability space... DIE

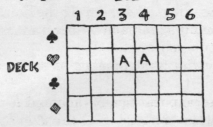

The line along the top is divided into 6 equal bits
to represent the numbers on the die. The line down
the side represents the four suits in a deck. The main
rule of probability spaces is that the chances of the
outcomes on each side must be equal. With a fair
dice, the chance of any number turning up is $\frac{1}{6}$ so
they are all the same. The pack of cards has 13 in
each suit so each suit has $\frac{13}{52} = \frac{1}{4}$ chance of turning up,
so they are all the same too and the probability
space works. Incidentally, this probability space
would *not* work with Riverboat Lil's pack of cards
because it has two extra aces of diamonds. Not only
does it cause diamonds to turn up slightly more often
than they should, Lil's pack also causes quite a lot of
broken windows and flying chairs in the Last Chance
Saloon so keep your head down if you're passing.

Each square on the diagram represents one of the possible outcomes, so to work out the chances there are two steps:

- See how many squares on the diagram correspond to the result you want.
- Divide by the total number of squares on the diagram.

In our diagram, the squares marked A represent the results when the card is a heart and the die is 3 or 4. There are only two of them, and so we divide this by the total number of squares which is $6 \times 4 = 24$. This gives the chance as $\frac{2}{24}$ or $\frac{1}{12}$.

See if you can use the diagram to tell what are the chances of picking a black card and throwing a 3 or higher?

Answer: You should find there are 8 squares that represent the useful results, so the chance is $\frac{8}{24}$ which is $\frac{1}{3}$.

Urgum, Grizelda and Hunjah's shoot-out

Heads down everybody because this one is nasty!

The three barbarian leaders have been having a furious argument about whose mum's cooking is stinking the whole street out. The only way to settle their differences is with a three-way duel to the DEATH. (Or until it hurts a lot.)

Each barbarian has a cannon and they stand on three hills in a triangle. The trouble is that Urgum can hit his target nearly every time, Grizelda can hit her target half the time and Hunjah hardly ever hits his target at all. To make it fair, they let Hunjah fire first, then Grizelda and then Urgum and they keep taking turns until one one person is left.

So there's Hunjah taking his first shot, but who should he aim at to give himself the best chance of surviving?

Suppose he aims at and shoots Urgum. Then he has a 50% chance of Grizelda shooting him next.

Suppose he aims at and shoots Grizelda. It's very likely that Urgum will then shoot him!

Amazingly enough, Hunjah's best option is for him to shoot into the air away from the others!

Grizelda is then bound to try and shoot Urgum because he is more dangerous. If Grizelda misses then Urgum will try and shoot her because she is more dangerous. Either way, Hunjah will end up with just one opponent rather than two so his chances will be slightly better!

You can try this game out. Draw a picture of Urgum, Grizelda and Hunjah (or put three little figures on the table) and get a die.

- Choose who Hunjah is (or isn't) aiming at and throw the die. If it lands on "1" then Hunjah has killed his target!
- Choose who Grizelda is aiming at and throw the die. If it lands on 1, 2 or 3 then Grizelda has killed her target.
- Choose who Urgum is aiming at and throw the die. If it lands on 1, 2, 3, 4 or 5 then Urgum kills his target.

Keep going until only one barbarian survives, then have a completely wild celebration party with lots of leaping about and shouting and things getting knocked over. (Which is very similar to the dying stages of a game of Monopoly.)

Other odds

People love working out the chances of things happening, and it makes for some rather amazing results even if we've no idea what sums were involved!

- Your chance of being struck by lightning: 1 in 600,000.
- The chances of a big asteroid hitting Earth in the next year: 1 in 100,000.
- Your chances of falling under a bus: 1 in 1,000,000.

- The chances of a bus falling under you: 1 in 1,000,000,000,000,000,000,000.
- The chances of meeting the dead rock star Elvis Presley alive and working in your local laundrette: 1 in 10,000. (At least, that's what some people believe…)

Lightning never strikes twice

This old saying suggests that if something unlikely has happened, you can be assured it won't happen again in the same place or to the same person. It's an interesting bit of superstition and it led soldiers in wartime to shelter in bomb craters because they thought that it was very unlikely for the same place to be bombed a second time. Hmmm…

Imagine you're on the station platform described on page 26 and there are TWO pigeons preparing to fire.

You might think it's impossible for them both to splat you. Wrong! These events have the same chance of 1 in 200 and, more importantly, they are independent. Even if the first pigeon did get you, the second one could still get you too and the chances of being splatted by this pigeon are exactly the same as for the first one. Rotten luck, but not impossible.

The same goes for lightning. If you're unlucky enough to have been zapped once in your life, don't go climbing the Eiffel Tower in a thunderstorm thinking you've had your bit of bad luck and can't ever be zapped again. In fact, an American Park Ranger called Roy Sullivan was zapped by lightning seven times, but amazingly he survived them all. Can you imagine what the chances of that must be?

Spots, spinners and silver dollars

Here are two games that seem fair until you play them! We'll get Binky along to help us demonstrate them.

MORE GAMES, EH? GOOD SHOW!

The three spots

You need three identical white bits of card. On one of them you draw a black spot on both sides, and on another you just draw a black spot on one side. The spots should all look exactly the same.

SPOT ON BOTH SIDES

BLANK ON OTHER SIDE

BLANK ON BOTH SIDES

Here's how the game works:

SHUFFLE UP THE CARDS AND TURN THEM OVER AS MUCH AS YOU LIKE. THEN PICK ONE AND PUT IT ON THE TABLE...

RIGHTO!

It looks like an even chance, doesn't it? But in fact, as long as you always say that the bottom side is the same as the top side, you will be right two times in three!

Suppose you play the game, but aren't allowed to see which card Binky has picked. As two of the three cards have matching sides, the chances of the top side and underneath being the same are $\frac{2}{3}$. But because Binky can see one side of the card, he has fooled himself into thinking that there is an even chance. It's worth trying this trick out, even if it's just on yourself!

The sneaky spinners!

Look at this diagram of four spinners:

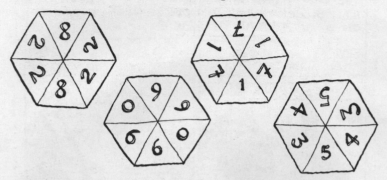

If you add up the numbers on each spinner, you'll find they all make the same total: 24. (If you want to play the game, copy these shapes on to card. Cut them out carefully then put a dead match through the middle of each one, held in place with blu-tack.)

The game is simple:

The secret is to look at the biggest number on each spinner which is 5, 6, 7 or 8. Whichever spinner Binky chooses, we choose the one with the next number up, so...

If Binky chooses "5" we choose "6".
If Binky chooses "6" we choose "7".
If Binky chooses "7" we choose "8".
But if Binky chooses "8" we choose "5".

Amazingly enough, with this game we will win about twice as many times as Binky does.

Three silver dollars

And finally, let's catch up with a sneaky little game that Riverboat Lil plays in The Last Chance Saloon. We've seen three coins being tossed before, but pay close attention to this because it's clever ... very clever!

Can you see why the chance is NOT even, despite Lil's clever little speech?

Answer: Tossing three coins has 8 possible outcomes, just like Pongo's teas and coffees on page 67. Only 2 of these outcomes are all heads or all tails, so the chance is 2 out of 8 or $\frac{1}{4}$. Where Lil gets sneaky is when she talks about the third coin. Which coin is supposed to be the third one?

The Great Rhun's golden egg

MANY THOUSANDS OF YEARS AGO THERE DID LIVE THE GREAT RHUN OF JEPATTI. HE WAS THE RICHEST GOVERNOR OF THE GOLDEN PROVINCES AND THIS IS JUST ONE MORE TALE OF HOW HE CAME BY HIS FABULOUS WEALTH...

The Rhun was well known for his love of a wager and many affluent merchants would call by in the hope of availing themselves of some of his ridiculous wealth. One such merchant was Lemeile the Spicebringer and the game he was invited to play was simple. The Rhun called upon the Grand Cahjoon to bring in a bag fashioned from crimson velvet. Inside the bag it was understood that there were ten eggs, nine of which were quite ordinary but the tenth had been coated with the finest gold leaf. Neither player was allowed to see inside the crimson bag lest they gained an advantage as to the position of the golden egg. However, prior to the game Lemeile was invited to feel the bag gently and check that there were indeed ten eggs present.

The Cahjoon explained that the two players were to take turns in removing an egg from the bag. Whosoever removed the golden egg would win.

The stakes were high. Lemeile put forward every item of value in his possession even unto his huge silky trousers. In return the Rhun put up every coin in his colossal coffers, and offered his daughter's hand in marriage. (The rest of his daughter was already married to someone else.) As a courtesy to his guest the Great Rhun even allowed Lemeile to pick the first egg.

"And so I give you a one in ten chance of winning immediately," explained the Rhun.

The Spicebringer took his turn, but the egg was plain.

"And now my chance of winning is one in nine," said the Rhun, but the egg he drew was as plain as the first. "How fun it is that the chance increases with each draw!" he remarked.

"And now for your turn the chance is one in eight."

For a second time the Spicebringer dipped his hand into the bag and again he pulled a plain egg. As did the Rhun. For a third and fourth time they both picked an egg, and each egg was plain. There were only two eggs left in the bag and again it was the turn of the merchant. His hand quivered uncontrollably over the bag.

"Relax," smiled the Great Rhun. "After all, you now have an even chance, wouldn't you say?"

"Even indeed," replied the merchant who was sweating profusely. "And yet in a moment one of us will be ruined."

"Let's up the stakes a little," suggested the Rhun, rolling up his sleeve. "Cahjoon, summon the Ghinji!"

The Grand Cahjoon clapped his hands and at once the three-tongued mutant bounded into the room brandishing a triple-edged sword.

"Ghinji, watch the bag!" commanded the Rhun. "Chop off the hand that draws the plain egg!"

The merchant was almost in a state of collapse.

"Your turn," said the Rhun. "And roll your sleeve up."

The merchant summoned all his courage and dipped into the bag. The Ghinji drooled as Lemeile withdrew his hand and then slowly opened his fingers. The egg was plain. The Ghinji raised his sword.

"My chance seems to have increased to a certainty!" chuckled the Rhun.

"No!" screamed the merchant. "Please, I beg of you! Take my money and let me go."

"But I haven't had my turn yet," said the Rhun.

"Just take all I have," begged Lemeile leaping out of his trousers and hurriedly draping them around the Grand Cahjoon's neck. "Let me be gone intact."

"Better let him go, I suppose," muttered the Rhun. "Just when it was getting fun too."

Off ran the merchant. The Rhun reached into the bag.

"Ghinji!" called the Rhun. "Treat! Open wide!"

The Ghinji tipped his head back and his slobbering jaw almost reached the floor.

"I must say with the deepest and humblest

respect, Great Rhun," said the Grand Cahjoon as he eyed up the pile of booty left by the merchant, "you are one jammy tinker."

"Jammy nothing," said the Rhun as he removed the tenth *plain* egg from the bag and tossed it into the delighted mutant's mouth.

So what do you think now?

We've seen how chance affects every aspect of our lives, but there's one big sum still left to do: the chances of life itself.

Scientists have tried to get the answer by desperately scanning the skies for the merest hint of other life forms, but space is so big and we're so small it's hardly surprising that they haven't had much luck. So just like tons of other problems, it's all down to the maths wizards to work out the *probability* of other life existing.

It's a toughie. There are umpteen different factors to consider and the odds on each one are almost impossible to estimate. However, us Murderous Mathsy types don't scare easily so we'll try our own special way of thinking about it.

Suppose you were just a ghost and you were floating round the universe looking for some functioning life-form to inhabit. How likely is it that you'd find one?

- To start with, any life-form that we might understand would need a solid planet or moon to exist on.

I COULD MURDER A CUP OF TEA...

So how many solid planets and moons are there? They've only recently started to find a few outside the solar system, but it's fair to assume that there must be billions and billions of them. This is GOOD NEWS.

- If we find a solid planet or moon, will it be too hot or too cold?

Will it have the all-important water available? If we check our own solar system we find that out of all the 9 planets and the 50-odd moons, only Earth and possibly a couple of the other moons would qualify. This makes the odds only about 5%. This is DISAPPOINTING NEWS.

- What other ingredients do we need for life? As life on Earth is all very much carbon-based, then let's assume that's all we need. Luckily there seems to be plenty of carbon about so this is GOOD NEWS.

- If the conditions are suitable and all the right ingredients are there, what are the chances of life starting up? This is a tricky one. Some people say this is about as likely as dropping a 1,000,000 piece jigsaw out of an aeroplane, and all the bits miraculously fitting together when they hit the ground. DISASTROUS NEWS.

- If everything else has gone to plan at some point and life forms were created, what are the chances that they are alive NOW? Maybe they came alive and found nothing to eat so died immediately. Or maybe they got squashed by a falling rock or fell into a lava pit.

Maybe they lived well for a few million years but then a meteor wiped them all out … life is a very risky business! NOT VERY ENCOURAGING NEWS.

So as you float around being a ghost, you'll realize that finding any sort of life form to inhabit – even a purple space mushroom – could become extremely tedious.

But you can relax. It was only a silly maths problem, and in fact you are NOT a ghost because you are here on a solid planet with water and everything else needed to live, and what's more you've just proved that you have the fantastic intelligence needed to comprehend a whole bookful of murderous maths. In terms of life in the universe, you have really beaten the odds!

So – do you feel lucky?